NEW YORK
PERFORMANCE
ASSESSMENT

10

Approaching Common Core Assessments with Confidence

By Carol Jago

In order to get good at anything, you need to practice. Whether the goal is to improve your jump shot, level up in a video game, or make the cut in band tryouts, success requires repeated practice on the court, computer, and field. The same is true of reading and writing. The only way to get good at them is by reading and writing.

Malcolm Gladwell estimates in his book *Outliers* that mastering a skill requires about 10,000 hours of dedicated practice. He argues that individuals who are outstanding in their field have one thing in common—many, many hours of working at it. Gladwell claims that success is less dependent on innate talent than it is on practice. Now I'm pretty sure that I could put in 10,000 hours at a ballet studio and still be a terrible dancer, but I agree with Gladwell that, "Practice isn't the thing you do once you're good. It's the thing you do that makes you good."

Not just any kind of practice will help you master a skill, though. Effective practice needs to focus on improvement. That is why this series of reading and writing tasks begins with a model of the kind of reading and writing you are working towards, then takes you through practice exercises, and finally invites you to perform the skills you have practiced.

Once through the cycle is only the beginning. You will want to repeat the process many times over until close reading, supporting claims with evidence, and crafting a compelling essay is something you approach with confidence. Notice that I didn't say "with ease." I wish it were otherwise, but in my experience as a teacher and as an author, writing well is never easy.

The work is worth the effort. Like a star walking out on the stage, you put your trust in the hours you've invested in practice to result in thundering applause. To our work together!

Unit 1 Argumentative Essay
Big Issues

STEP 1 ANALYZE THE MODEL

The Debate Over When to Begin the School Day

Read Source Materials

STEP 2 PRACTICE THE TASK

The Debate Over Businesses Banning Teenagers

Read Source Materials

STEP 3 PERFORM THE TASK

The Debate Over Raising the Minimum Driving Age

Read Source Materials

Unit 2 Informative Essay
Great Adaptations

STEP 1 ANALYZE THE MODEL

How have birds adapted to their environments?

Read Source Materials

Unit 3 Literary Analysis
Inspirations

STEP 2 PRACTICE THE TASK

How can real events inspire poetry and other writing?

Read Source Materials

STEP 3 PERFORM THE TASK

How do our life experiences change us?

Read Source Materials

© Houghton Mifflin Harcourt Publishing Company • Image Credits: ©Creativemarc/Shutterstock; ©Houghton Mifflin Harcourt; ©Creativa/Shutterstock

Unit 4 Mixed Practice
On Your Own

Big Issues

Argumentative Essay

STEP
1 ANALYZE THE MODEL

Evaluate an argumentative essay concerning proposed changes to the start time for high schools.

STEP
2 PRACTICE THE TASK

Write an argumentative essay that takes a precise position regarding businesses having the right to ban teenagers from their establishments.

STEP
3 PERFORM THE TASK

Write an argumentative essay that takes a precise position regarding raising the minimum driving age.

How do we relate to and interact with other people—friends, enemies, neighbors, strangers, and those with whom we disagree? And how does age affect the way that people act or react in difficult or controversial situations?

No doubt you have been involved in many arguments—squabbles with your friends, disagreements with siblings, and those times when you have tried to convince someone about something you want. This kind of informal, conversational give-and-take is different from a formal argument.

IN THIS UNIT, you will learn how to write an argumentative essay that is based on your close reading and analysis of several relevant sources. You will learn a step-by-step approach to stating a claim, and then organize your essay to support your claim in a clear and logical way.

The Debate Over When to Begin the School Day

You will read:

▶ **TWO INFORMATIONAL ARTICLES**
from Sleep Deprivation in Teenagers

from School Start Time and Sleep

You will analyze:

▶ **A STUDENT MODEL**
We Need Our Sleep!

Source Materials for Step 1

The texts on these two pages were used by Mr. Goldberg's student, Bao Chen, as sources for his essay "We Need Our Sleep!" As you read, make notes in the side columns and underline information that you find useful.

NOTES

No sleep - makes their test scores down dramatically

jobs, hw, activities can prevent kids from getting their sleep.

If they don't get sleep - their moods can be different and will have difficulty focusing

from

Sleep Deprivation in Teenagers

by Ramon Ruiz

For the past 30 years, Dr. Smith and his research team have studied sleep patterns in high school students. These studies of 14- to 18-year-olds have shown that when students learn something new and are then deprived of REM sleep, their test scores go down dramatically. This comes as no surprise to Dr. Smith, who knows that certain kinds of memory are sensitive to sleep loss. He theorizes that, if 14- to 18-year-olds are susceptible to such effects when prevented from getting enough sleep, younger children might be affected more severely. Students in grade school need between 9 and 10 hours of sleep for optimal learning.

Although it may vary from person to person, most teenagers need 9.5 hours of sleep. Unfortunately, extracurricular activities, after-school jobs, and homework may result in teenagers getting no more than 7.5 hours of sleep a night. If teens consistently do not get enough sleep, their moods can be affected. They will have difficulty performing and reacting as usual.

Medical Journal Today **Volume 9, Issue 4 (2014), page 212**

1. Analyze   2. Practice   3. Perform

from
School Start Time and Sleep

The National Sleep Foundation
www.sleepfoundation.org

"Early to bed, early to rise makes a man healthy, wealthy and wise," said Ben Franklin. But does this adage apply to teenagers? Research in the 1990s found that later sleep and wake patterns among adolescents are biologically determined; the natural tendency for teenagers is to stay up late at night and wake up later in the morning. This research indicates that school bells that ring as early as 7:00 a.m. in many parts of the country stand in stark contrast with adolescents' sleep patterns and needs.

Evidence suggests that teenagers are indeed seriously sleep deprived. A recent poll conducted by the National Sleep Foundation found that 60% of children under the age of 18 complained of being tired during the day, according to their parents, and 15% said they fell asleep at school during the year.

On April 2, 1999, Rep. Zoe Lofgren (D-CA), introduced a congressional resolution to encourage schools and school districts to reconsider early morning start times to be more in sync with teens' biological makeup. House Congressional Resolution 135 or the "ZZZ's to A's" Act would encourage individual schools and school districts all over the country to move school start times to no earlier than 8:30 a.m.

NOTES

Teenagers stay up late and wake up in the morning

Children say that they are tired - and sleep in class

Encourage schools to start no earlier than 8:30 to be more sync with the teens sleep times

Discuss and Decide

You have read two sources about teenagers and sleep. Without going any further, discuss your thoughts about high schools starting an hour later each morning. Use details from the texts to support your position.

Analyze a Student Model for Step 1

Read Bao's argumentative essay closely. The red side notes are the comments that his teacher, Mr. Goldberg, wrote.

Bao Chen
Mr. Goldberg
English 10
October 28

We Need Our Sleep!

Beep! You shut off the alarm. It's 6:00 a.m.—time to get ready for high school—but you don't have the energy. Eventually you stagger into your first class at 7:15. Is this the morning you want to experience for the rest of your school career? No. Recent studies show that 85% of American teens aren't getting the sleep they need. Although some may prefer classes ending in the early afternoon, school should start later.

Getting up too early has serious consequences. Studies from the American Psychological Association show that the frontal lobe (the section of the brain in charge of learning ability and memory) is still developing in many adolescents (Carpenter 42). Disturbing REM (rapid eye movement) sleep can slow the development of this vital portion of the brain. This can result in much lower test scores (Ruiz 212). Our principal said, "Students in first period classes tend to score lower on standardized math tests than their peers who take the same classes later in the day." We should be as concerned about disturbing students' natural sleep patterns as we are about skipping school.

Side notes (handwritten)

hook is interesting
claim is clear (which side)

Nice hook. The issue and your claim are both clear. Your audience is clear.

story reveals the problem and ends w the solution at the ending

Strong circular structure with an anecdote here to reveal the problem and then a revised anecdote at the end of the essay with the solution

nice—the way the writer wrote it

Well-constructed paragraph

follows everything stated in intro

Logical follow-up to your introduction

good reasoning evidence

Valid reason, supported by sufficient evidence

where the evidence is coming from is clear

Clear text citations woven into your writing

many evidence is used

Variety of evidence used, including example, expert opinion, facts, and commonly accepted beliefs

Moreover, Trent University studies on sleep deprivation have shown that grades aren't the only thing that might improve. Additional sleep can positively affect a student's attitude (Blakeslee A11). My grandfather says that he went to school later in the morning and students were happier. With students' moods boosted, teachers and students would be less stressed.

Some people may argue that teenagers who need to get up before dawn can adapt to the situation by going to bed earlier. Adults who start work early often compensate by adjusting the time they go to sleep. In this way, they get enough rest. This would seem to make sense, however, the claim ignores what we've learned about adolescent development. Research in the 1990s confirmed that later sleep and wake patterns in teens are biologically determined. (Carskadon et al. 871). Although the research did not assess whether teens could adapt their sleep cycles to early school start times, Congress is currently considering the "ZZZ's to A's Act," which would encourage schools to start after 8:30 a.m. ("School Start Time and Sleep").

Now imagine that morning again. It's 7:00 a.m. You say to yourself, "Wow, I feel great, and I've got time to get ready." Just one hour can make a difference in your mood and your day.

Works Cited

Blakeslee, Sandra. "For Better Learning, Researchers Endorse 'Sleep on It' Adage." *New York Times* 7 Mar. 2000: A11. Print.

Carpenter, Siri. "Sleep Deprivation May Be Undermining Health." *Monitor on Psychology* 32.9 (2001): 42. Print.

Carskadon, Mary, Amy Wolfson, Christine Acebo, Orna Tzischinsky, and Ronald Seifer. "Adolescent Sleep Patterns, Circadian Timing, and Sleepiness at a Transition to Early School Days." *SLEEP* 21.8 (1998): 871–881. Print.

Ruiz, Ramon. "Sleep Deprivation in Teenagers." *Medical Journal Today* 9.4 (2014): 212. Print.

"School Start Time and Sleep." *Sleep News.* The National Sleep Foundation, n.d. Web. 6 Oct. 2015.

Side annotations:

You use an effective transition to create cohesion and signal the introduction of another reason. Your language is formal and non-combative. You remain focused on your purpose.

Used another word to tell the reader you are starting a new paragraph

You address an opposing claim that is likely to occur to your audience. Your answer to the opposing claim is effective because you explore a strength before answering it with valid evidence.

gave a good reason before giving evidence

Smooth flow from beginning to end. Clear conclusion restates your claim. Your evidence is convincing. Excellent use of conventions of English.

good essay, clear essay, evidence was persuasive, excellent words used

Discuss and Decide

Did Bao convince you that school should start an hour later? If so, which evidence was the most compelling?

Terminology of Argumentative Texts

Read each term and explanation. Then look back at Bao Chen's argumentative essay and find an example to complete the chart.

Term	Explanation	Example from Bao's Essay
audience	The **audience** for your argument is a group of people that you want to convince. As you develop your argument, consider your audience's knowledge level and concerns.	"American teens aren't getting the sleep they need although some prefer classes ending in the early afternoon"
purpose	The **purpose** for writing an argument is to sway the audience. Your purpose should be clear, whether it is to persuade your audience to agree with your claim, or to motivate your audience to take some action.	"encourage school to start after 8:30 a.m"
precise claim	A **precise claim** confidently states your viewpoint. Remember that you must be able to find reasons and evidence to support your claim, and that you must distinguish your claim from opposing claims.	"Although some may prefer classes ending in the early afternoon, school should start later"
reason	A **reason** is a statement that supports your claim. (You should have more than one reason.) Note that you will need to supply evidence for each reason you state.	"Sleep can slow the development of the vital portion of the brain. This can result in much lower test scores"
opposing claim	An **opposing claim**, or **counterclaim,** shares the point of view of people who do not agree with your claim. Opposing claims must be fairly presented with evidence.	"some people may argue that teens who need to get up before dawn can adapt to the situation by going to bed earlier"

1. Analyze   2. Practice   3. Perform

PRACTICE THE TASK

The Debate Over Businesses Banning Teenagers

You will read:

▶ **A NEWSPAPER AD**
Munchy's Promise

▶ **A BUSINESS ANALYSIS**
Munchy's Patrons, July and October
Munchy's Monthly Sales,
July–October

▶ **AN OPINION POLL**
Percentage of Age Groups That Are
Comfortable Around Teenagers

A STUDENT BLOG
Munchy's Bans Students!

▶ **A NEWSPAPER EDITORIAL**
A Smart Idea Can Save a Business

You will write:

▶ **AN ARGUMENTATIVE ESSAY**
Take a precise position regarding
businesses having the right to ban
teenagers from their establishments.

Source Materials for Step 2

AS YOU READ Analyze the ad, business analysis, opinion poll, blog, and editorial. Think about the information, including the data contained in the sources. Annotate the sources with notes that help you decide where you stand on the issue regarding businesses having a right to ban teenagers from their establishments.

Source 1: Newspaper Ad

from *Springfield Daily Mail,* **12 November 2014: 19**

Munchy's Promise

Aren't you tired of eating lunch surrounded by noisy high school students?

Aren't you fed up with endless cellphone conversations, loud music, messy tables?

Aren't you infuriated seeing teenage students taking over every restaurant downtown?

We promise that you'll have the quiet lunch you deserve, because MUNCHY's has the solution!

No music!
No cellphones!
NO STUDENTS!

Mr. Joe "Munchy" Jones and his team will make sure you get the midday break that YOU deserve!

Munchy's
321 Main Street
555-5252

Use this coupon for a **10% discount** on your next "quiet lunch."

COME TO A "QUIET LUNCH" AT MUNCHY'S!
From noon to 3 pm, Monday through Friday, we will be a teen-free zone!

Close Read

1. What assumptions is Mr. Jones making about teenagers?

_____

2. What assumptions is he making about adults?

_____

1. Analyze   2. Practice   3. Perform

Source 2: Business Analysis

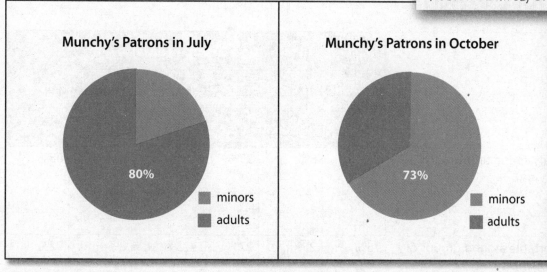

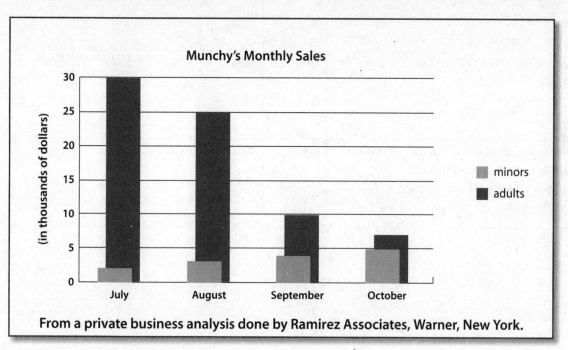

From a private business analysis done by Ramirez Associates, Warner, New York.

Discuss and Decide

1. Explain the data shown in the pie charts.

2. What is the implication of the data shown in the bar graph?

3. Explain the relationship between the two forms of data.

Source 3: Opinion Poll

Percentage of Age Groups That Are Comfortable Around Teenagers

from Public Opinion Surveys, Inc., Minneapolis, MN, published at
www.publicopinionsurveys.com, January 11, 2013

	Age Group (Years)					
QUESTION	12–18		19–65		66 and up	
	Yes	No	Yes	No	Yes	No
Do you regularly spend time around people aged 12–18?	92%	8%	35%	65%	12%	88%
Are you comfortable around groups of people aged 12–18?	75%	25%	27%	73%	8%	92%
Do you think people aged 12–18 have poor manners?	21%	79%	48%	52%	67%	33%
Have you ever been around a group of people aged 12–18 that caused trouble that needed to be resolved by the police or an adult in charge?	53%	47%	30%	70%	9%	91%

1. Analyze   2. Practice   3. Perform

Interpreting Charts, Graphs, and Tables

To understand information in graphic format and to use it in an argumentative essay, you must interpret it correctly. Keep the following in mind:

Study the Title

The title indicates the basic information contained in the chart or graph. For example, the two different pie charts on page 11 indicate that they contain the same information (Munchy's Patrons) but in different months (July, October).

Note the Legend, Axis Labels, Column Headings, Row Descriptions

The legend for pie charts and bar graphs often use colors to indicate the information that is shown. For example, the bar graph on page 11 uses different colors to indicate monthly sales to minors and monthly sales to adults. It also shows that the bars indicate thousands of dollars in monthly sales (vertical axis) and that the bars show sales for different months (horizontal axis).

In the table on page 12, the column headings indicate the age of the group of people who were asked questions and their answers. The row descriptions identify the questions that were asked.

Compare Information for Different Groups or Time Periods

The intent of most charts, graphs, and tables is to show trends or to make comparisons. You need to study the information presented to see if you can identify a trend or make an important comparison.

For example, when you compare the information in the pie charts, you can see a big difference in the percentages of minors and adults in the two different months. The bar graph indicates a trend of reduced sales from the summer to the fall months. The table allows you to see the differences in how comfortable people of different ages feel around teenagers.

Draw Conclusions Based on the Information

A strong argumentative essay draws conclusions from reliable evidence. This means that you must decide what the information means and what the trends or comparisons indicate. Answer the questions below to practice drawing conclusions.

Discuss and Decide

1. What does the information in the table on page 12 show?

2. Why is the information in the table important in helping you establish a position on the issue?

Source 4: Student Blog

Enter your email address:

[   ]

Subscribe me!

Profile

This blog is run by the Student Council of Springfield High School, and it discusses issues and events that affect all the students of SHS and its community.

Labels

unfair
high school
students
lunch
action

Previous entries

November 15, 2014

 Like   Dislike

Munchy's Bans Students!

In today's newspaper, the old-fashioned lunch spot known as Munchy's, popular among students of this institution, announced its new "quiet lunch"—without students!

The restaurant took out a full-page ad in the newspaper to advertise its new rule banning students from noon to 3 P.M. The ad claimed that high school students are noisy, play loud music, and are on their cellphones all the time.

Obviously, this piece of advertising was crafted to attract business people, who are allegedly quieter and need a more relaxing environment. Newsflash! Business people are ALWAYS on their cellphones, having loud conversations!!! The last time I was at Munchy's, ALL the noise came from business people who were on their cells or arguing. It comes down to who spends more money. There are not many options in town other than Munchy's: a couple of unhealthy fast-food places, and our school cafeteria.

Age discrimination is an outrage and a violation of our civil rights! Let's get together in front of Munchy's next Wednesday and pass out leaflets to inform the public about this unfair regulation.

This new policy of Munchy's is shortsighted. As Audra Morales, president of the Chamber of Commerce, said in an interview, "Our members have found that building relationships with younger customers leads to customers who continue to patronize their establishments as adults."

Please come and bring your signs and loud voices!

SCSHS Blog. **Student Council of Springfield High School.**

Close Read

Does the lunch hour ban on teens guarantee a "quiet lunch"? Cite evidence in the blog text to support your answer.

_____

1. Analyze   2. Practice   3. Perform

Source 5: Newspaper Editorial

Springfield Daily Mail

November 17, 2014

B 4

A Smart Idea Can Save a Business

In these days of economic uncertainty, the last thing business owners want to do is drive customers away. In fact, Article III, 173-79 of the Springfield bylaws states that exclusion of any person seeking to patronize an establishment for legitimate reasons is prohibited. However, we are witnessing the hardships that many stores and restaurants are facing in our city, fighting to break even and stay open. In order to help the economy, the Mayor has stressed the relationship between a thriving business district and property values—something that affects all of us. The Mayor's office is trying to attract more people downtown by creating pedestrian-only zones and giving business owners tax breaks if they promote the city's tourist attractions.

But most of the time, municipal help is not enough, and rather than hang a "going out of business" sign on their front door, some business owners try to take the bull by the horns and make their own rules in order to improve their revenue. This week, we applaud the marketing strategy of Joseph Jones, who took out a full-page ad announcing a policy change at Munchy's, his popular eatery. After identifying a decrease in profits during the school months, Mr. Jones realized that many of his faithful, adult, wealthier, customers— mostly business people from the offices that surround his restaurant downtown—were staying away from Munchy's due to the havoc high school students cause every day at lunchtime. In fact, teens are to a restaurant as weeds are to a garden. Therefore, he proclaimed the hours between noon and 3 P.M. "quiet lunch" time, during which students will be banned from the premises. Mr. Jones's solution is supported by Professor Battaluri of Essex University. In an October 2, 2014, interview she said, "In my opinion, the data gathered by my team clearly indicates an increase in monthly sales when restaurants focus on satisfying the needs of adult customers." This regulation will clearly encourage business people—who spend more money at lunch and need a break from their busy days—back into the restaurant.

We wish Mr. Jones and the team at Munchy's the best of luck, and we congratulate them once more for their creative idea!

Discuss and Decide

1. What smart idea does the editorial applaud?

2. What reasons are given to endorse Mr. Jones's new policy?

Respond to Questions on Step 2 Sources

These questions will help you analyze the sources you've read. Use your notes and refer to the sources in order to answer the questions. Your answers to these questions will help you write your essay.

1 Evaluate the sources. Is the evidence from one source more credible than the evidence from another source? When you evaluate the credibility of a source, examine the expertise of the author and/or the organization responsible for the information. Record your reasons in the chart.

Source	Credible?	Reasons
Newspaper Ad Munchy's Promise		
Business Analysis		
Opinion Poll Percentage of Age Groups . . .		
Student Blog Munchy's Bans Students!		
Newspaper Editorial A Smart Idea Can Save a Business		

2 **Prose Constructed-Response** If you were supportive of "Munchy" Jones's position, which sources would you use to defend your opinion? Explain your rationale, citing evidence from the sources.

_____

_____

3 **Prose Constructed-Response** Examine the data in the Business Analysis. Explain to what extent the blog and the newspaper editorial could rely on or use these data.

_____

_____

Types of Evidence

Every reason you offer to support the central claim of your argument must be upheld by evidence. It is useful to think ahead about evidence when you are preparing to write an argument. If the evidence to support your claim is limited or unconvincing, you will need to revise your claim. The evidence you provide must be relevant, or related to your claim. It must also be sufficient. Sufficient evidence is both clear and varied. Using evidence from several different sources shows the prominence of the issue and your idea about it. If evidence is pulled from only one source, it calls the credibility of the argument into question. Types of evidence found in these sources include anecdotes, commonly accepted beliefs, examples, expert opinion, and facts.

Use this chart to help you vary the types of evidence you provide to support your reasons.

Types of Evidence	What Does It Look Like?
Anecdotes: personal examples or stories that illustrate a point	
Commonly accepted beliefs: ideas that most people share	
Examples: specific instances or illustrations of a general idea	
Expert opinion: statement made by an authority on the subject	
Facts: statements that can be proven true, such as statistics or other numerical information	

Write an argumentative essay that takes a precise position regarding businesses having the right to ban teenagers from their establishments.

Planning and Prewriting

Before you draft your essay, complete some important planning steps.

Claim ➡ Reasons ➡ Evidence

 You may prefer to do your planning on a computer.

Make a Precise Claim

1. Do you agree or disagree with Munchy's? That is, should a business have the right to ban teenagers?　　　　　yes ☐　　no ☐

2. Review the evidence on pages 10–15. Do the sources support your position?　　　　　yes ☐　　no ☐

3. If you answered *no* to Question 2, you can either change your position or do additional research to find supporting evidence.

4. State your claim. It should be precise. It should contain the issue and your position on the issue.

> **Issue:** Some businesses are banning teenagers from their establishments.
>
> **Your position on the issue:** _____
>
> **Your precise claim:** _____

State Reasons

Next, gather support for your claim. Identify several valid reasons that justify your position.

Reason 1	Reason 2	Reason 3

Find Evidence

You have identified reasons that support your claim. Summarize your reasons in the chart below. Then complete the chart by identifying varied evidence that supports your reasons.

Relevant Evidence: The evidence you plan to use must be *relevant* to your argument. That is, it should directly and factually support your position.

Sufficient Evidence: Additionally, your evidence must be *sufficient* to make your case. That is, you need to supply enough evidence to convince others.

Varied Evidence: Finally, be sure your evidence is *varied*. It should come from multiple sources and represent different types of evidence—anecdote, commonly accepted beliefs, examples, expert opinion, and/or facts.

Short Summary of Reasons	Evidence
Reason 1	Relevant? _____ Sufficient? _____ Varied? _____
Reason 2	Relevant? _____ Sufficient? _____ Varied? _____
Reason 3	Relevant? _____ Sufficient? _____ Varied? _____

Address Opposing Claims

You have written out your precise claim, reasons that support it, and evidence that supports those reasons. Now you need to anticipate opposing claims and address them so that your argument is the most persuasive. To present the strongest argument, review evidence that shows the strength of the opposing claim as well as its weakness. Remember that every argument, no matter how strong, will have an opposing claim.

Once you've identified an opposing claim, select one or more ways to refute it. These include:

▶ Challenging the credibility of the source supporting the opposing claim

▶ Noting that the opposing claim is true only in certain circumstances

▶ Noting that the opposing claim addresses only certain facts, not all facts

▶ Identifying the opposing claim as biased

▶ Explaining the possible biases influencing the opposing claim

Follow these steps:

Opposing Claim(s)	Evidence
Identify the Opposing Claim(s) Review your precise claim. Look back at the source material to identify opposing claims. How do these opposing claims help you identify weaknesses in your argument? Write out one or more opposing claims clearly.	
Select Ways to Refute the Opposing Claim(s) Think carefully about the opposing claims. Are there problems with: • credibility? • truth in all circumstances? • addressing only certain facts? • bias? Write notes on the best way to refute the claim.	

Finalize Your Plan

Whether you are writing your essay at home or working in a timed situation at school, it is important to have a plan. You will save time and create a more organized, logical essay by planning the structure before you start writing.

Use your responses on pages 18–20, as well as your close reading notes, to complete the graphic organizer.

▶ Think about how you will grab your reader's attention with an interesting fact or anecdote.

▶ State your precise claim.

▶ Identify the issue and your position.

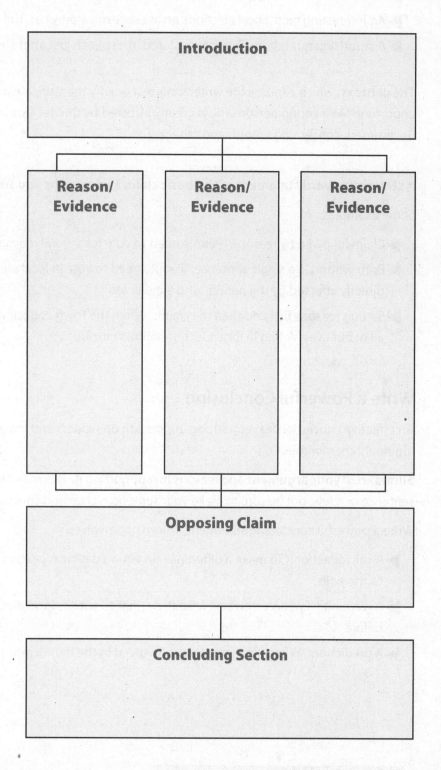

Introduction

Reason/ Evidence   **Reason/ Evidence**   **Reason/ Evidence**

▶ List the likely opposing claim and how you will counter it.

Opposing Claim

▶ Restate your claim.

Concluding Section

Write a Clear and Engaging Introduction

An effective introduction includes:

A hook that engages readers and grabs their attention. Some examples:

> ▶ A rhetorical question: "What if no one voted in local elections?"

> ▶ An anecdote: "When my grandfather voted for the first time in the 1950s, . . ."

> ▶ An interesting fact: "Local elections on average draw only half the number of voters . . ."

> ▶ A surprising quotation: "Our mayor stated in a speech just after she took office in 2015 . . ."

The context, which explains the writer's interest or why the issue is especially important: "As a young person who is greatly affected by the decisions of our local government concerning schools and other issues . . ."

A straightforward statement of the basic claim and reasons you support it.

Some examples:

> ▶ Claim followed by reasons: "People need to vote for several reasons. First, . . ."

> ▶ Both written in a single sentence: "People need to vote in local elections because their lives are directly affected by the people who are elected."

> ▶ Stating reasons first and then the claim: "When the town council votes to raise tax rates, it affects all of our lives. Voting in local elections allows citizens . . ."

Write a Powerful Conclusion

An effective conclusion leaves a strong impression on readers and makes your argument memorable.

Summarize your argument and reasons for supporting it. This may be a single sentence or a few, but be sure to make your sentences clear and concise.

Write a powerful concluding statement. This might involve:

> ▶ A call for action: "To make a difference on voting day next year, volunteer to help get people to the polls."

> ▶ A warning: "If people don't exercise their right to vote in local elections, it won't be long before . . ."

> ▶ A prediction: "When more people are involved in the democratic process, our town will . . ."

Cite Your Sources

A credible argumentative essay is based on reliable sources that are cited within the essay and listed at the end. Many teachers and organizations support the format used by the Modern Language Association (MLA). This style is used in the sample essay on pages 6–7.

Create a "Works Cited" List

Place Citations within Your Essay Be sure to include citations in your essay each time you use a direct quote or an important piece of background information. If the author's name appears in the same sentence, include just the page number in parentheses right before the ending punctuation. If the author's name doesn't appear in the sentence, list the author's last name before the page number.

Get Help Online As with many other modern tasks, there is software that can help you create the correct citations within your essay and list the sources at the end. If you have Internet access, several options are available at http://mlaformat.org/mla-format-generator/. It is always best to understand the process and guidelines, whether you use an online generator or complete the process on your own. Follow the steps below to learn about the process and complete essential tasks.

Make Notes on Each Source You'll need the following information to create citations with a generator or to complete them yourself (information for websites and print sources differs slightly):

- Author(s)
- Publication title and type of publication (newspaper, book, website, etc.)
- Publisher
- Date of publication
- Page numbers, especially if there are multiple pages, if you are quoting directly from the publication, or if you are using specific rather than general information, such as statistics or dates

Create Your "Works Cited" List Use the following bulleted suggestions to format and perfect your list:

- List all of the sources you have used in your essay in the Works Cited list.
- The author is always listed with the last name first. The list is then arranged by alphabetical order of the first word in each entry (usually the author's last name).
- Check with your teacher to see if he or she would like the actual Web address (URL) for an Internet source to appear in the citation. (The MLA no longer requires it.)
- Use these guidelines for creating your Works Cited list for the sources on pages 10–15:

   Newspaper: Author(s). "Title of Article." *Title of Periodical* Day Month Year: pages. Medium of publication.

   Website: Editor, author, or compiler name (if available). *Name of Site.* Version number. Name of institution/organization affiliated with the site (sponsor or publisher), date of resource creation (if available). Medium of publication. Date of access.

Draft Your Essay

As you write, think about:

▶ **Audience:** Your teacher and your classmates

▶ **Purpose:** Demonstrate your understanding of the requirements of an argumentative essay.

▶ **Style:** Use a formal and objective tone that isn't defensive.

▶ **Transitions:** Use words such as *furthermore, consequently, nevertheless,* and *on the contrary* to create cohesion, or flow.

Revise

Revision Checklist: Self Evaluation

Use the checklist below to analyze your writing.

 If you drafted your essay on a computer, print it out to evaluate it more easily.

Ask Yourself	Tips	Revision Strategies
Does the introduction grab the audience's attention and include a precise claim?	Draw a wavy line under the attention-grabbing text. Bracket the claim.	Clarify the context. Add an attention grabber. Check that the order you use to state the claim and supporting reasons is the most convincing. Think about which sentences can be combined for a smoother introduction.
Do at least two valid reasons support the claim? Is each reason supported by relevant and sufficient evidence?	Underline each reason. Circle each piece of evidence, and draw an arrow to the reason it supports.	Add reasons or revise existing ones to make them more valid. Add relevant evidence to ensure that your support is sufficient.
Do transitions create cohesion and link related parts of the argument?	Put a star next to each transition.	Add words, phrases, or clauses to connect related ideas so writing flows smoothly.
Are the reasons presented in an order and with transitions that help you to sound convincing? Are connections clear?	Number the reasons in the margin, ranking them by their strength and effectiveness.	Rearrange the reasons into a more logical order of importance.
Are opposing claims fairly addressed, discussed, and refuted?	Put a plus sign by any sentence that addresses an opposing claim.	Add sentences that identify and address those opposing claims.
Does the concluding section restate the claim, summarize major points, and possibly include a warning, a prediction, or a call for action?	Put a box around the restatement of your claim.	Add a sentence that restates your claim.
Have you cited all your facts and evidence correctly?	Circle the information that comes from another source. Add a parenthetical citation for each circled item.	List all sources in your Works Cited list using MLA format.

Revision Checklist: Peer Review

Exchange your essay with a classmate, or read it aloud to your partner. As you read and comment on your classmate's essay, focus on logic, organization, and evidence—not on whether you agree with the author's claim. Help each other identify parts of the draft that need strengthening, reworking, or a new approach.

What To Look For	Notes for My Partner
1. Does the introduction clarify the context, contain an attention grabber, and include the claim and supporting reasons arranged in a clear and convincing manner?	
2. Do at least two valid reasons support the claim? Is each reason supported by relevant and sufficient evidence?	
3. Do transitions and the precise use of vocabulary words help connect ideas and link related parts of the essay?	
4. Are the reasons stated in body paragraphs valid, mindful of counterclaims, sufficient, and arranged in the most persuasive manner possible?	
5. Are opposing claims fairly acknowledged and refuted?	
6. Does the concluding section restate the claim, summarize major points, and possibly include a warning, a prediction, or a call for action?	
7. Are the sources cited accurately and formatted properly?	

Edit

 Edit your essay to correct spelling, grammar, and punctuation errors.

NOTES

The Debate Over Raising the Minimum Driving Age

You will read:

▶ **TWO INFORMATIONAL ARTICLES**
Traffic Safety Facts

Teenage Driving Laws May Just Delay Deadly Crashes

You will write:

▶ **AN ARGUMENTATIVE ESSAY**
Take a precise position regarding raising the minimum driving age.

2008 Data

TRAFFIC SAFETY FACTS

from the National Highway Traffic Safety Administration (www.nhtsa.gov)

AS YOU READ *Analyze the data presented in the articles. Look for evidence that supports your position on raising the minimum driving age, or evidence that inspires you to change your position.*

NOTES

There were 205.7 million licensed drivers in the United States in 2007 (2008 data not available). Young drivers, between 15 and 20 years old, accounted for 6.4 percent (13.2 million) of the total, a 4.8-percent increase from the 12.6 million young drivers in 1997. In 2008, 5,864 15- to 20-year-old drivers were involved in fatal crashes—a 27-percent decrease from the 7,987 involved in 1998. Driver fatalities for this age group decreased by 20 percent between 1998 and 2008. For young males, driver fatalities decreased by 19 percent, compared with a 24-percent decrease for young females (Table 1). Motor vehicle crashes are the leading cause of death for 15- to 20-year-olds (based on 2005 figures, which are the latest mortality data currently available from the National Center for Health Statistics). In 2008, 2,739 15- to 20-year-old drivers were killed and an additional 228,000 were injured in motor vehicle crashes.

10

Source (pages 28–31): "Traffic Safety Facts: Young Drivers." www-nrd.nhtsa.dot.gov. National Highway Traffic Safety Administration. Undated.

Close Read

How many fewer 15- to 20-year-old drivers were involved in fatal crashes in 2008 than in 1998? Cite textual evidence in your response.

_____

_____

_____

1. Analyze   2. Practice   3. Perform

Graph

**Driver Fatalities and Drivers Involved in Fatal Crashes Among
15- to 20-Year-Old Drivers, 1998–2008**

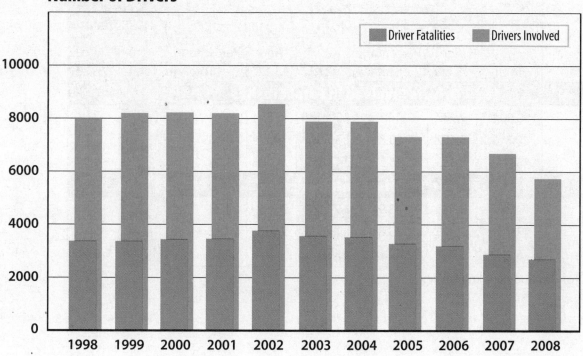

Number of Drivers

Close Read

Is this a true statement? *In 2002, more than half of fatal crashes among 15- to
20-year-olds killed someone other than the driver.* Use the data in the graph and
cite evidence in your response.

_____

_____

_____

_____

Table 1

Involvement of 15- to 20-Year-Old Drivers in Fatal Crashes by Sex, 1998 and 2008

| | 1998 | | | 2008 | | | Percentage Change, 1998–2008 | |
	Total	Age 15–20	Percentage of Total	Total	Age 15–20	Percentage of Total	Total	Age 15–20
Drivers Involved in Fatal Crashes								
Total	56,604	7,987	14.1	50, 186	5,864	11.7	-11	-27
Male	40,816	5,652	13.8	36,881	4,174	11.3	-10	-26
Female	15,089	2,335	15.5	12,568	1,688	13.4	-17	-28
Driver Fatalitites								
Total	24,743	3,431	13.9	24,175	2,739	11.3	- 2	-20
Male	17,992	2,476	13.8	18,694	2,010	10.8	- 4	-19
Female	6,750	955	14.1	5,473	727	13.3	-19	-24

Note: Total includes unknown sex.

NOTES

In 2008, 12 percent (5,864) of all drivers involved in fatal crashes (50,186) were young drivers age 15 to 20 years old, and 14 percent (1,429,000) of all drivers involved in police-reported crashes (10,081,000) were young drivers.

Close Read

What can you conclude about the driving behavior of male and female drivers?

_____

_____

_____

_____

1. Analyze   2. Practice   3. Perform

Table 2

Population and Drivers Involved in Fatal Crashes by Age Group, 2008

	Age Group (Years)							
	15–20	21–24	25–34	35–44	45–54	55–64	65–69	70+
Population (Percent)	8.5	5.5	13.5	14.0	14.6	11.1	3.7	9.1
Drivers Involved in Fatal Crashes (Percent)								
–Single-Vehicle	14.0	13.1	20.9	16.9	15.5	10.3	2.8	6.2
–Multi-Vehicle	10.4	9.2	19.0	18.3	17.8	12.4	3.5	9.3
–All Fatal Crashes	11.9	10.8	19.8	17.8	16.8	11.5	3.2	8.1

Among 15- to 20-year-old drivers involved in fatal crashes in
20 2008, 30 percent (291) of those who did not have valid operator's
licenses at the time of the crash also had previous license suspensions
or revocations (Table 3).

Table 3

Young Drivers Involved in Fatal Crashes by Previous Driving Record and License Compliance, 2008

	License Compliance				Total (5,864)*	
	Valid (4,882)		Invalid (970)			
Driving Record	Number	Percent	Number	Percent	Number	Percent
Previous Recorded Crashes	748	15.5	96	9.9	845	14.4
Previous Recorded Suspensions and Revocations	433	9.0	291	30.0	727	12.4
Previous DWI Convictions	63	1.3	37	3.8	100	1.7
Previous Speeding Convictions	1,017	21.1	135	13.9	1,154	19.7
Previous Other Harmful or Moving Convictions	877	18.2	182	18.8	1,060	18.1

* Includes 72 drivers with unknown license status. Note: Excluding all drivers with unknown previous records.

Close Read

Cite evidence from the text and graphics to support this statement: *Driver fatalities for 15- to 20-year-olds decreased 20% between 1998 and 2008.*

Source 2 : Informational Article

Teenage Driving Laws
May Just Delay Deadly Crashes

by Anahad O'Connor from *The New York Times* website, September 14, 2(

AS YOU READ *Pay attention to cause-and-effect relationships between changing licensing laws for teenage drivers and the rate of fatal crashes. Jot down comments or questions about the text in the side margins.*

NOTES

A nationwide study shows that tougher licensing laws for teenage drivers have reduced deadly accidents among 16-year-olds, but with an unintended consequence: increasing the fatal crash rate among 18-year-olds.

Over the last two decades, many states have put in place strict teenage driving laws, with graduated driver's license programs that require young drivers to meet certain restrictions before they obtain a full license. While the rules vary by state, they generally set a minimum age for earning a driver's permit or license and require a
10 set number of supervised hours behind the wheel, and some prohibit driving with fellow teenagers, ban night driving or require at least six months of instruction before a driver's test. Over all, the tougher laws—which most states began adopting in the mid-1990s—have been credited with a 30 percent drop in highway fatalities among teenagers.

But "most of the prior studies on graduated driver licensing have only looked at 16-year-olds," said Scott Masten, a researcher with California's Department of Motor Vehicles and the lead author of the current study. "When you do that you go, 'Wow, these programs are
20 saving lives,'" he said.

Discuss and Decide

Before reading the rest of the selection, discuss what sorts of reasons could account for the phenomenon mentioned in the first paragraph.

1. Analyze   2. Practice   3. Perform

To get a broader perspective, Dr. Masten and his colleagues looked at data on fatal crashes involving 16- to 19-year-olds that occurred over a 21-year period, beginning in 1986. "When you look at the bigger picture across 18- and 19-year-olds, it looks like we're offsetting those saved crashes," he said. "In fact, 75 percent of the fatal crashes we thought we were saving actually just occurred two years later. It's shocking."

The study, published Wednesday in The Journal of the American Medical Association, found that since the first graduated driver programs were instituted, there have been 1,348 fewer deadly crashes involving 16-year-old drivers. But at the same time, there have been 1,086 more fatal crashes that involved 18-year-olds. The net difference is still an improvement, Dr. Masten said, but not quite the effect that many had assumed.

"The bottom line is there is still a net overall savings from introducing all these programs," he said. "So we are saving teen drivers over all, but it's not nearly what we thought it would be."

Dr. Masten strongly suspects that the reason for the increase in deadly crashes among 18-year-olds is that many teenagers, rather than deal with the extra restrictions for 16- and 17-year-olds, are simply waiting to get a license until they turn 18, and skipping the restrictions altogether. As a result, a greater proportion of inexperienced drivers hit the road at 18. He pointed out that when California instituted its tougher driving laws for teenagers, the proportion of 16- and 17-year-olds getting licenses to drive dropped while the numbers at 18 and 19 did not.

But the authors also suggested another hypothesis: that teenagers going through graduated driver license programs are not getting as much practical driving experience when they have "co-drivers." In other words, while having adult supervision in the car reduces risk, it also protects teenage drivers so much that they miss out on learning experiences that can be gleaned only by driving alone, like knowing what it means to be fully responsible for a vehicle and knowing how to "self-regulate."

Discuss and Decide

How have teenage driving laws changed? What are some of the results of these changes? Cite textual evidence in your response.

"Even though we want you to learn by driving with your parents, it's really different from the sorts of things you learn when you're driving on your own," Dr. Masten said. "The whole thing about learning to drive is you need to expose yourself to crash risk to get experience."

60   In an editorial that accompanied the study, researchers with the Insurance Institute for Highway Safety, a nonprofit group financed by insurance companies, said the findings raised a "serious issue" that policy makers should take note of. They pointed out that one of the states with the toughest programs for teenage drivers is New Jersey, where all first-time drivers under 21 have to adhere to graduated driver restrictions.

"New Jersey's approach has been associated with significant reductions in the crash rates for 17- and 18-year-olds and virtually eliminates crashes among 16-year-olds, without adversely affecting
70   crash rates for 19-year-old drivers," the authors wrote.

But in a twist, New Jersey's tough laws may have just shifted the effect to 21-year-olds, similar to the way tough restrictions on 16- and 17-year-olds were followed by a spike in deadly crashes among 18-year-olds in other states, Dr. Masten said. In New Jersey, a study of deadly crashes did not look specifically at 21-year-olds; they were mixed into a larger group of 20- to 24-year-olds. But the research still found a 10 percent increase in deadly crashes in that group after New Jersey's tougher graduated driver licensing program was instituted, suggesting that 18-, 19- and 20-year-olds may be waiting out the
80   tough restrictions there as well.

Close Read

What general principle does New Jersey's experience suggest about driving restrictions and age?

_____

_____

_____

1. Analyze   2. Practice   3. Perform

Other researchers have also found that the reason the rate of crashes among teenagers is so high—they account for 10 times as many crashes as middle-aged drivers—is not that they are reckless, but that they make simple mistakes, like failing to scan the road, misjudging driving conditions and becoming distracted. Some of these problems can be addressed through what experts call narrative driving: having adult drivers point out to teenage passengers examples of unsafe driving and explain to them how they are dealing with distractions on the road.

90 Lack of sleep can also be a major factor in teenage crashes. A study in the Journal of Clinical Sleep Medicine this year found that teenagers who started school earlier in the morning had higher crash rates.

Close Read

Provide evidence from the article that supports the position of allowing teenagers to drive at age 16. Then provide evidence that supports the position of *not* allowing teenagers to drive at 16.

Pro	Con
Support Allowing 16-Year-Olds to Drive	**Against Allowing 16-Year-Olds to Drive**

Respond to Questions on Step 3 Sources

These questions will help you think about the sources you've read. Use your notes and refer to the sources in order to answer the questions. Your answers to these questions will help you write your essay.

1 Is the evidence from one source more credible than the evidence from another source? When you evaluate the credibility of a source, examine the expertise of the author and/or the organization responsible for the information. Record your reasons.

Source	Credible?	Reasons
Informational Article Traffic Safety Facts		
Informational Article Teenage Driving Laws May Just Delay Deadly Crashes		

2 **Prose Constructed-Response** What point about teen driving is raised in both the article "Teenage Driving Laws May Just Delay Deadly Crashes" and the data from "Traffic Safety Facts"? Why is this point important to address when making an informed decision about teen driving? Support your answer with details and statistics.

_____

_____

_____

3 **Prose Constructed-Response** Does the bar graph in "Traffic Safety Facts" support or contradict the information in the article "Teenage Driving Laws May Just Delay Deadly Crashes"? Use details from the article and the graph to support your answer.

_____

_____

_____

Part 2: Write

ASSIGNMENT

You have read about traffic accidents caused by teens. Now write an argumentative essay in which you take a precise position regarding raising the minimum driving age. Support your claim with details from what you have read.

Plan

Use the graphic organizer to help you outline the structure of your argumentative essay.

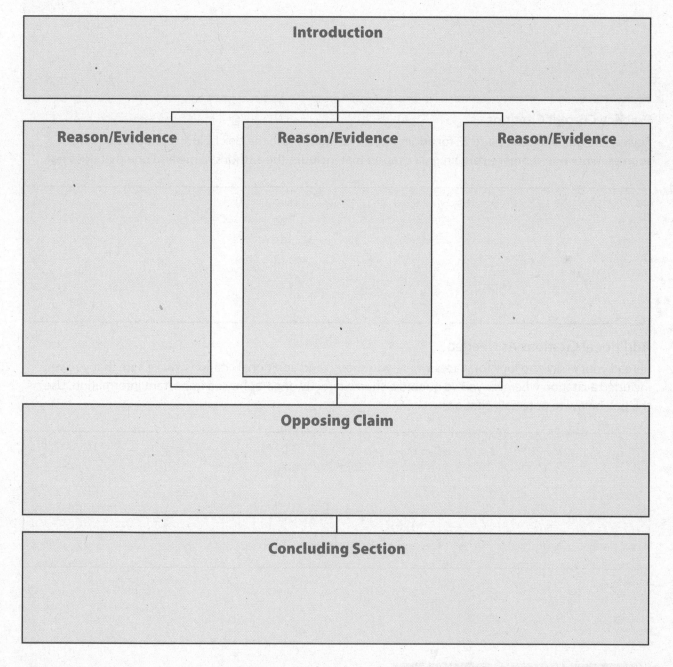

Introduction

Reason/Evidence

Reason/Evidence

Reason/Evidence

Opposing Claim

Concluding Section

Cite Additional Sources

Citing an adequate number of sources is essential to a strong argumentative essay. Reread your essay and revise it to include any additional citations that are needed. This will give readers a chance to judge the reliability of your sources and how well they support your precise position. Review the information you learned on pages 28–35 and put it into practice below.

Create Your Works Cited List

If you haven't done it already, use the box below to list the sources on pages 28–35 in MLA format.

Practice Correct Citations

Review the guidelines on page 23 for adding in-text citations. Use the box below to practice adding sources. Write one sentence containing a citation that includes the author's name and one that does not.

Additional Citations As Needed

Reread your essay and look for places where you should add additional citations. Make sure that you've included a citation wherever you've quoted a source directly or paraphrased important information. Use the box below to note new citations.

Draft

 Use your notes and completed graphic organizer to write a first draft of your argumentative essay.

Revise and Edit

 Look back over your essay and compare it to the Evaluation Criteria. Revise your essay and edit it to correct spelling, grammar, and punctuation errors.

Evaluation Criteria

Your teacher will be looking for:

1. *Statement of purpose*

- ▶ Is your claim specific?
- ▶ Did you support it with valid reasons?
- ▶ Did you anticipate and address opposing claims fairly?

2. *Organization*

- ▶ Are the sections of your essay organized in a logical way?
- ▶ Is there a smooth flow from beginning to end?
- ▶ Is there a clear conclusion that supports the argument?
- ▶ Did you stay on topic?

3. *Elaboration of evidence*

- ▶ Is the evidence relative to the topic?
- ▶ Is there enough evidence to be convincing?
- ▶ Did you cite all of your sources using a proper format?

4. *Language and vocabulary*

- ▶ Did you use a formal, noncombative tone?
- ▶ Did you use vocabulary familiar to your audience?

5. *Conventions*

- ▶ Did you follow the rules of grammar usage as well as punctuation, capitalization, and spelling?
- ▶ Did you cite all your sources, both in the text of your essay and in a Works Cited list, using the correct MLA formats?

NOTES

Great Adaptations

Informative Essay

STEP 1

ANALYZE THE MODELS

Evaluate two informative essays about the albatross and the cormorant.

STEP 2

PRACTICE THE TASK

Write an informative essay about deep-sea creatures.

STEP 3

PERFORM THE TASK

Write an informative essay on adaptations made by wildlife in Australia.

An informative essay, also called an expository essay, is a short work of nonfiction that informs and explains. Unlike fiction, nonfiction is mainly written to convey factual information, although writers of nonfiction shape information in a way that matches their own purposes. Nonfiction writing can be found in newspaper, magazine, and online articles, as well as in biographies, speeches, movie and book reviews, and true-life adventure stories.

The nonfiction topics that you will read about in this unit describe animals in very different environments. The information in the sources is factual.

IN THIS UNIT, you will analyze information from two articles on native and invasive new animals in Australia. You will select and organize relevant facts and ideas to convey information about a topic, and you will end your essay by summarizing ideas or providing a concluding statement.

© Houghton Mifflin Harcourt Publishing Company • Image Credits: ©Digital Vision/Getty Images

STEP 1

ANALYZE THE MODEL

How have birds adapted to their environments?

You will read:

▶ **AN INFORMATIONAL ARTICLE**
Don't Start Without a Plan

You will analyze:

▶ **TWO STUDENT MODELS**
Two Water Birds: The Albatross and the Cormorant

Are Most Water Birds Similar?

Source Materials for Step 1

Ms. Mehta's students read the following text to help them plan and write an informative essay. As you read, underline information that you find useful.

NOTES

Don't Start Without a Plan

You probably have already had challenging writing assignments that required you to research, then plan and write an informative essay. Whether the subject is a science, history, or another nonfiction topic, you need to decide in advance how you will organize your information and present it effectively. Don't just start *somewhere* and keep on writing until you have met the page requirement.

When you write an informative essay, the parts should *relate* to each other in a clear way to support your topic. A framework for writing can help you focus and manage information and ideas.

Framework for an Informative Essay
Introduction
Hook your reader's interest and clearly identify your subject. Make your topic and the central idea about the topic clear.
Body
Discuss each sub-topic that supports your central idea in one or more paragraphs and support each sub-topic with multiple details, including facts, examples, and quotations.
Conclusion
Bring your essay to a close by tying your ideas together. Summarize or restate your central idea(s) or draw conclusions.

Developing Your Topic

When you develop ideas in the body of your essay, you may want to use a text structure such as comparison and contrast to organize information. If you use comparison and contrast, you can follow two different types of organization:

© Houghton Mifflin Harcourt Publishing Company

1. Analyze   2. Practice   3. Perform

1. Point-by-Point If you were to write an essay comparing or contrasting small colleges and large universities, you might organize the essay using a point-by-point structure. To do this, the body of your essay would have a paragraph or two comparing and contrasting the student body of small colleges and large universities. You might then write a paragraph or two comparing and contrasting class size at small colleges and large universities. You might finish the body of the essay with one or two paragraphs that compare or contrast the organizations and clubs at small colleges and large universities.

Point	Small College	Large University
1. **Student Body**		
2. **Class Size**		
3. **Organizations**		

Discuss the first point of comparison or contrast for both small colleges and large universities, then move on to the second point.

2. Subject-by-Subject If you use this organizational structure, your essay will have one or two paragraphs discussing the student body, class size, and organizations within small colleges, followed by one or two paragraphs discussing those same three points as they relate to large universities. Discuss all the points about small colleges before moving on to large universities.

Subject	Student Body	Class Size	Organizations
1. **Small College**			
2. **Large University**			

You may also want to use **narrative description** to develop aspects of your topic. Narrative description is about real people, events, or procedures. You can use narrative description to provide an account of historical events or to add detail to a scientific procedure. General descriptions won't help your reader see your subject. Use concrete sensory details expressed with precise and vivid nouns, verbs, and modifiers. Use the following structures to organize your descriptions.

Organizing Description	
Chronological Order	**Order of Importance**
Describe details in the order in which they occur, especially in descriptions of events.	Start with the most important detail and work toward the least important, or vice versa.

Discuss and Decide

What descriptive details would likely be included in the essay on colleges and universities?

Analyze Two Student Models for Step 1

Tyrell used comparison-contrast to develop the content of his essay. Read his essay closely. The red side notes are comments made by his teacher, Ms. Mehta.

Tyrell's Model

Point	Albatross	Cormorant
1. Habitat	Lives far out at sea	Never ventures too far from land
2. Behavior	Solitary	Social
3. Special Adaptations	Adapted for life on and over the sea	Adapted to hunt underwater

Tyrell Jackson
Ms. Mehta, English
December 3

Two Water Birds:
The Albatross and
the Cormorant

The intro sets up what you are comparing and contrasting.

The albatross and the cormorant are two birds that spend their time in, on, and over the water. While both are winged creatures, their physical makeups are different. Each bird is designed to be better suited for its environment and survival tasks.

Habitat

"On the other hand" is a good phrase to indicate a contrast.

For example, albatrosses, with their huge wingspan (the biggest of any bird—up to eleven or twelve feet wide) are rarely seen on land. They spend most of their lives far out to sea, riding the air currents or, when there is not enough wind, sitting on the surface of the water (Marlin). Cormorants, on the other hand, are coastal birds that never venture too far from land. Because their feathers are not waterproof, they need to get dry after spending time in the water diving for food. You will often see a group of cormorants sitting on a dock or rocky pier with their wings outstretched, drying out (Williams).

1. Analyze   2. Practice   3. Perform

Behavior

The albatross is for the most part a solitary creature. It only gets together with others during breeding season, on remote islands out at sea. The female lays one egg per year; after the chick learns to fly, it heads out to sea and doesn't return to land until it is ready to breed, five to ten years later (Marlin). Cormorants are almost the opposite. They are very social—feeding, traveling, and roosting in groups. The chicks in a cormorant colony are also social; they spend the day together in a "crèche,"[1] returning to their own nests for food (Benoit 301).

A cormorant takes advantage of a raft to scout for food.

Special Adaptations

The albatross is adapted for life on and over the sea. Because it spends so much time far from land, it drinks seawater, using a special gland located above the eyes to lower the water's salt content (Farley, Chilton, and Ruiz). Thanks to several adaptations, an albatross can ride ocean air currents for hours without once flapping its wings. For example, special tubes in its nostrils measure airspeed; a locking mechanism in the shoulder means it doesn't need to use any muscles (or energy) to keep its wings extended.

---

[1] **crèche:** a group of young animals gathered together in one place, where adult animals can care for and protect them

Bones are a good comparison point, especially because you compare more than just the albatross and cormorant here.

Meanwhile, cormorants have evolved to be speedy and agile underwater hunters. The bones of most birds are hollow, but a cormorant's are solid so it can more easily dive down and stay submerged (Williams). Its short, muscular wings help it to "fly" underwater. It can adapt its focus for both above and underwater vision ("Cormorant Count").

As the saying goes, "To each his own." Albatrosses and cormorants each have evolved the physical and behavioral traits they need to survive and succeed.

Works Cited

Benoit, James R. *Millions on the Wing: A History of the Cormorant.* Portland, ME: Velaquez, 2003. Print.

"Cormorant Count." *FCOB Blog.* Ocean Birdwatchers of Fairhaven County, n.d. Web. 23 Nov. 2015.

Farley, Shannon, Brandon Chilton, and Marika Ruiz. "Albatross Fact Sheet." *Fishing Environment Quarterly* 24.6 (2001): 35. Print.

Marlin, Shannon. "Albatrosses: a Life at Sea." *New Brunswick Shore Patrol Online.* Nov. 2014. Web. 18 Nov. 2015.

Williams, Muro. "Birds of the Oceans." *Compendium of Marine Avian Knowledge.* Port Fiske, FL: Avian Knowledge, Inc., 2001. 101–125. Print.

Discuss and Decide

Did the structure of Tyrell's model follow the text structure described in the source material? Explain.

1. Analyze   2. Practice   3. Perform

Jenna's essay covers the same topic as Tyrell's, but she chose to develop her comparison-contrast essay using a subject-by-subject structure instead of point-by-point.

Jenna's Model

Subject	Habitat	Behavior	Special Adaptations
Albatrosses	mostly sea	independent	drink salt water
Cormorants	close to land	live in groups	hunt underwater

Jenna O'Leary
Ms. Mehta, English
December 5

Are Most Water Birds Similar?

It's easy to assume that birds that live around the water are very similar. Why wouldn't they be? They are living in the same environment. But a little research shows that water birds can be as different as night and day. An albatross and a cormorant are both considered water birds, but other than that, they differ in just about every other way.

Dispelling a common myth—this is a strong way to hook your reader.

Albatrosses

With the exception of the first few months of its life and short periods when it is breeding, an albatross spends its entire life alone at sea. Females lay a single egg on a remote ocean island, and after a chick matures in several months, it flies away to spend the next five to ten years gliding over ocean waters, feeding on squid and sometimes garbage from ships. After breeding, adults fly away again and return to their solitary life above the ocean waters ("albatross").

Mentioning that albatrosses sometimes feed on garbage is interesting and shows that they have to search hard for food.

This photograph shows the wingspan of a gliding albatross.

For centuries, sailors have marveled at the sight of a solitary albatross gliding on the ocean winds for hours at a time without even moving its wings. How do these huge birds, with a wingspan of eleven to twelve feet, larger than any other bird, stay in the air so long (Rossiter, Lee, and Jimenez)? They have special tubes in their nostrils that help them measure airspeed, and their shoulders lock in a special way so they don't have to use any energy to keep their wings extended for gliding. Because life at sea doesn't allow access to fresh water, an albatross has a salt gland above its eyes that lets it drink seawater. The salt in the seawater that an albatross drinks moves through its blood stream into the gland. Then the salt is pushed through its nostrils and runs down its bill to form a drop at the end. Finally, the albatross shakes its head to fling the salt back into the ocean (Rossiter, Lee, and Jimenez).

Cormorants

If you're near an ocean, you've probably seen cormorants as well. But these birds are extremely different from the albatross. They spend a large part of their life on land although they get their food by diving into the water for fish. Surprisingly, their feathers are not waterproof, so large groups are often seen in coastal areas with their wings spread out so they can dry (Mayhew 417).

They spend most of their time with other cormorants in a large group. Even their young chicks spend their days together in a group where the adults can feed and care for them ("cormorant").

Cormorants are so good at fishing that in some areas of Asia they have been trained to fish for people ("cormorant"). One reason they are so good at this is that there bones are solid, rather than hollow like most birds. This allows the cormorants to stay underwater and swim after they dive beneath the surface. Their eyes move separately, an adaptation that helps them see the movement of prey when they are both in and out of the water. However, cormorants aren't able to see a lot of details. Basically they dive, see if anything moves, and then catch it (Mayhew 422).

You have provided explicit details about both the albatross and the cormorant and included precise explanations on the significance of these details.

© Houghton Mifflin Harcourt Publishing Company

1. Analyze   2. Practice   3. Perform

Successful Species

Even though both albatrosses and cormorants live on or near the water and depend on it for food, they don't share many characteristics. Both have developed special characteristics that have allowed their species to thrive for thousands of years.

Works Cited

"albatross." *Encyclopædia Britannica. Encyclopædia Britannica Online.* Encyclopædia Britannica Inc., 2015. Web. 22 Nov. 2015.

"cormorant." *Encyclopædia Britannica. Encyclopædia Britannica Online.* Encyclopædia Britannica Inc., 2015. Web. 22 Nov. 2015.

Mayhew, Edward J. *Cormorants: A Misunderstood Bird.* Windburg, NH: Aquatex, 2008. Print.

Rossiter, Mary, Daniel Lee, and Manuel Jimenez. "Gliding the Wind: Life of the Albatross." *Marine Exploration Quarterly* 25.9 (2001): 56–58. Print.

Close Read

Why is a subject-by-subject text structure appropriate in this essay? Did it convey the information about the similarities and differences between water birds effectively?

_____

_____

_____

Terminology of Informative Texts

Read each term and explanation. Then look back and analyze each student model. Find an example to complete the chart. Finally, make a claim about which model was more successful in illustrating each term.

Term	Explanation	Example from Student Essays
topic	The **topic** is a word or phrase that tells what the essay is about.	
text structure	The **text structure** is the organizational pattern of an essay.	
supporting evidence	The **supporting evidence** is relevant quotations and concrete details that support the focus.	
domain-specific vocabulary	**Domain-specific vocabulary** is content-specific words that are not generally used in conversation.	
text features	**Text features** are features that help organize the text, such as: headings, boldface type, italic type, bulleted or numbered lists, sidebars, and graphic aids, including charts, tables, timelines, illustrations, and photographs.	

Prose Constructed-Reponse How do text features support the reader in learning about the topic of each essay? Support your claim by citing text evidence.

_____

_____

_____

1. Analyze   2. Practice   3. Perform

What adaptations allow deep-sea creatures to survive in extreme environments?

You will read:

▶ **A DATABASE**
Giant Squid (Architeuthis dux)

▶ **A SCIENCE ARTICLE**
Zombie Worms Drill Whale Bones with Acid

▶ **FIELD NOTES**
Trip into Blackness

▶ **AN INFORMATIONAL ARTICLE**
Deep-Sea Vents

You will write:

▶ **AN INFORMATIVE ESSAY**
What adaptations allow deep-sea creatures to survive in extreme environments?

Source Materials for Step 2

AS YOU READ You will be writing an informative essay about deep-sea creatures. Carefully study the sources in Step 2. Annotate by underlining and circling information that may be useful to you when you write your essay.

Source 1: Database

Giant Squid (*Architeuthis dux*)	
Anatomy	
Eyes	• Two eyes, each with a diameter of about 30 centimeters • Largest eyes of any animal on earth—great light-absorbing capacity
Funnel	• Located beneath the squid's body, or mantle • Pumps water, creating jet propulsion • Also serves to squirt ink, lay eggs, and expel waste
Feeding Tentacles	• Two tentacles, each up to 10 meters long • Tipped with hundreds of powerful, toothed suckers
Arms	• Eight arms, each about half the length of the feeding tentacles • Lined with thousands of powerful, toothed suckers • Guide squid's prey from its tentacles to its beak
Beak	• Located at the base of the feeding tentacles and arms • Slices prey into pieces for eating
Coloration	• At ocean surface: reddish orange to pink, with white mottling • In deep water: silvery to gold, depending on light source and angle
Ecology	
Range	• Worldwide • Rarely swims in polar or tropical seas—from distribution of specimens washed ashore
Habitat	• Probably prefers continental shelves and island slopes • 500 to 1,000 meters below ocean surface
Life Span	• Less than five years—as evidenced by growth rings in statoliths (mineralized organs that help the squid balance)
Reproduction	• Each individual probably mates only once
Diet	• Fish and other squids—from stomach contents of specimens washed ashore
Predators	• Sperm whales

Data compiled from "Giant Squid," by Clyde Roper & The Ocean Portal Team. Smithsonian National Museum of Natural History, undated Web. Retrieved Nov. 3, 2014.

Discuss and Decide

In what ways is the giant squid adapted for ocean living? Cite text evidence.

1. Analyze   2. Practice   3. Perform

Source 2: Science Article

Zombie Worms Drill Whale Bones with **Acid**

by Martha Ennis, Zoological Manager

Monterey, California—A mystery of one of the deep ocean's strangest creatures, the "zombie worms" of the *Osedax* family, has been solved. Analyzing the worms' tissues, scientists have discovered enzymes that secrete acid. This acid is crucial to the worms' remarkable life history.

In 2002, scientists at the Monterey Bay Aquarium Research Institute accidentally discovered these small worms at the bottom of the sea off the coast of California. The worms live on the skeletons of whales, which drift down to the ocean floor and constitute a rich source of nutrients. Somehow the worms drill into the bones and extract the stored nutrients, but scientists were puzzled because the worms have no body parts for physically drilling into the hard material. Indeed, the worms lack even a mouth and gut.

Instead, it turns out, the worms have developed a chemical strategy. A zombie worm attaches to a whale bone with special root-like structures. The skin cells of these structures produce an acid, which dissolves the bone, allowing the worm to extract the nutrients.

This is just one of *Osedax* worms' unusual adaptations for life on the ocean floor. In a classic example of symbiosis, the worms depend on internal bacteria to digest the fats and oils extracted from their whale-bone diet. And only female "zombies" grow to adulthood. Males, which live out their lives in the gelatinous tubes inside each female, never develop past larvae.

by Martha Ennis in *Monterey Bay Science Journal*, May 2013, p. 43.

Close Read

In what ways have zombie worms adapted to their environment? Cite evidence from the text.

_____

_____

Source 3: Field Notes

Trip into Blackness
by Arthur Jonssen, Marine Biologist
Mariana Trench, Pacific Ocean

11:20 A.M.	The weather is good, and the sea is calm, so our dive can proceed. After climbing into the submersible, we test the motors, batteries, robotic arms, and CO_2 scrubber. We review safety and emergency procedures with the ship's crew. Finally, the hatch is cranked shut, and we are ready to go.
11:52 A.M.	The submersible vibrates and tilts. I hear the squeal of the winch as we are lifted from the ship's deck and lowered into the ocean.
12:04 P.M.	As we descend, leaving the world of sunlight behind, the ocean shifts from green to aquamarine to an intense glowing blue, like the sky just after sunset. At a depth of about 500 meters, the panorama outside our bubble darkens and our visibility reduces rapidly.
12:15 P.M.	We're nearing the ocean floor at a depth of about 820 meters. The view outside is inky black. We keep the submersible's powerful lights off, for they might scare away our quarry. There! And there! We begin to see flashes of light—blue, yellow, red, and orange— as bioluminescent fish swim to avoid us.
12:48 P.M.	A large jellyfish swims by, flashing bright blue lights in a circular pattern that also turns on and off. Here is a good example of a bioluminescent "burglar alarm." If threatened by a predator, the jellyfish's striking display might scare the predator away. Or it might attract an even bigger predator that could then eat the fish that was about to eat the jellyfish.

Mariana Trench Blog. **Paine Institute of Oceanography. 6 Aug. 2013. Web.**

Close Read

Why does the jellyfish use bioluminescence as a defense, instead of remaining unseen in the darkness?

_____

1. Analyze 　　2. Practice 　　3. Perform

DEEP-SEA VENTS

by Amy Bliss

Location Near Antarctica in the Southern Pacific, 7,200 feet below the surface lies a chain of hydrothermal vents. This area has only recently been explored by a team of scientists. Because scientists are not adapted for deep-sea life, they used a remote-controlled underwater vehicle to explore the landscape.

Climate It's very hot and very cold at the same time. Hydrothermal vents form where two continental plates collide. Cold seawater pours into the earth's crust and encounters molten rocks. Water spewing back out of the vents' chimneys might reach 700°F. A few feet away, water is barely above freezing.

This unusual geology creates an extraordinary biological opportunity. When frigid water meets hot rock, chemical reactions produce an array of mineral compounds, which many organisms consider food. Down here, the web of life depends on chemistry, not photosynthesis.

Yeti Crabs Gathered in heaps around the thermal vents, white crabs wave their claws together in unison. Dubbed "yeti crabs" for their hairy chests and legs, these creatures are new to science. And they are clearly thriving, with up to 600 "yetis" living on each square meter (about 11 square feet) of their favored real estate. What do they eat? Scientists aren't sure but conjecture that mineral-eating bacteria might grow on the crabs' hairs and that the crabs might scoop up the bacteria.

From *Marine Research Today.* Volume 3. Issue 2 (2014): 98.

Discuss and Decide

How does the yeti crabs' diet work as an adaptation for their environment?

Preparing to Write a Comparison and Contrast Essay

Identifying Subjects and Points

When you write an informative essay that compares and contrasts facts, ideas, or events, your first job is to identify the subjects you will compare and contrast. You also need to identify the points or characteristics that can be compared or contrasted. In the model text on pages 49–51, there are subject headings that clearly identify the subjects: Albatrosses and Cormorants. In other cases, you may need to read a source closely and make notes, or look at other text features to identify the subjects covered. For example, if you look at the model text on pages 46–48, the title of the model, "Two Water Birds: The Albatross and the Cormorant," tells you what the text is about, but you need to read the model to find out what you will learn about the birds.

To truly compare and contrast, you need information on the same points for two or more subjects. For example, if you read two sources that each describe a different country, you need to be sure they cover similar points. If one describes the economy and people of a country, while the other describes the geography and government of a different country, you will not have enough information to write an essay that compares and contrasts how people live in the countries.

The model texts on pages 46–48 and 49–51 have different text structures, or are organized in different ways, but both of them compare and contrast the habitat, behavior, and special adaptations of albatrosses and cormorants. Therefore, you would certainly be able to use these essays as sources for your own essay about sea birds, but if you wanted to compare other points, you would need to look for other sources to support your ideas. When you are writing your own essays, you want to make sure you have enough information from your sources to support your ideas.

Using a graphic organizer like the one on the next page can help you determine the subjects of sources and the points they cover that might be compared. You can add more points to the chart as needed. Remember, you don't need to write much in the chart, just indicate points covered with a word or two.

1. Analyze   2. Practice   3. Perform

ASSIGNMENT

Using the sources on pages 54–57, write an informative essay that compares and contrasts the adaptations of two or more deep-sea creatures that allow them to live in their extreme environments.

Planning and Prewriting

Before you start writing, review your sources and start to synthesize, or integrate, the information they provide. Collect textual evidence in the chart below.

 You may prefer to do your planning on the computer.

Decide on Key Points

Summarize the main points and supporting evidence to include in your essay.

Characteristic	Subject 1	Subject 2	Subject 3
Point 1 _____ ☐ Alike ☐ Different			
Point 2 _____ ☐ Alike ☐ Different			
Point 3 _____ ☐ Alike ☐ Different			
Point 4 _____ ☐ Alike ☐ Different			
Point 5 _____ ☐ Alike ☐ Different			

Developing Your Topic

Before you write your essay, decide how to arrange your ideas. You can use one of the patterns of organization described below or come up with your own arrangement—whatever works best for your subject and evidence. Begin your essay with an introductory paragraph and end with a concluding paragraph.

Point-by-Point Discuss the first point of comparison or contrast for each subject, then move on to the second point. If you choose this organization, you will read across the rows of this chart.

Characteristic	Subject 1	Subject 2	Subject 3	
Point 1			→	If you use this organizational structure, your essay will have paragraphs comparing and contrasting the points in your chart. Your evidence should include details that support the points about each subject.
Point 2			→	
Point 3			→	
Point 4			→	
Point 5			→	

Subject-by-Subject Discuss all the points about your first subject before moving on to your other subjects. If you choose this method, you will be reading across the rows of this chart.

Subject	Point 1	Point 2	Point 3	Point 4	Point 5
Subject 1					→
Subject 2					→
Subject 3					→
If you use this organizational structure, your essay will start with one or two paragraphs about your first subject, followed by paragraphs containing points you choose to write about your other subjects.					

As you write, look back at the sources for examples of descriptive details that you can use in your essay.

Finalize Your Plan

Use your responses and notes from previous pages to create a detailed plan for your essay.

▶ Hook your audience with an interesting detail, question, or quotation to introduce your topic.

▶ Follow a framework like the one shown here to organize your points or subjects and supporting evidence.

▶ Include relevant facts, concrete details, and other textual evidence.

Reminder! Use your chosen text structure to develop your topic. The number of boxes in the graphic may need to be changed to work with your plan. Just make an expanded copy of the graphic on another sheet of paper.

▶ Summarize or restate your central idea(s).

▶ Provide a concluding statement that ties together your ideas or reflects on the information you've presented.

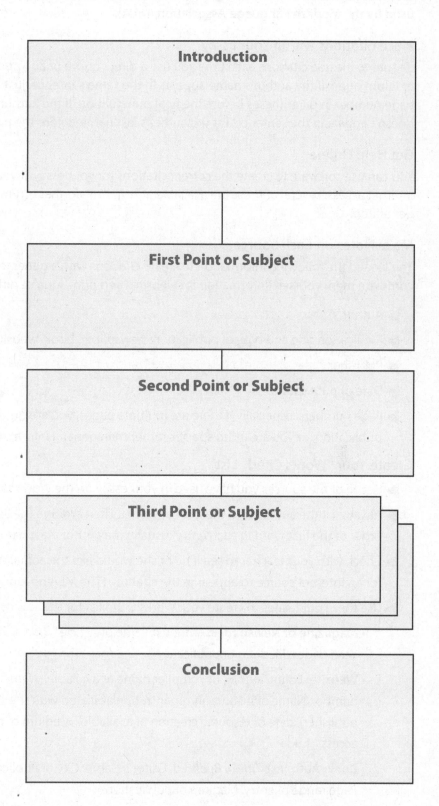

Introduction

First Point or Subject

Second Point or Subject

Third Point or Subject

Conclusion

Cite Your Sources

A credible informative essay is based on reliable sources that are cited within the essay and listed at the end. Many teachers and organizations support the format used by the Modern Language Association (MLA).

Place Citations within Your Essay

Be sure to include citations each time you use a direct quote or an important piece of information. If the author's name appears in the same sentence, just include the page number in parentheses before the final punctuation. If the author's name doesn't appear in the sentence, list the author's last name before the page number.

Get Help Online

You can use software to create the correct citations for your essay. If you have Internet access, several of these are available at http://mlaformat.org/mla-format-generator/.

Make Notes on Each Source

You'll need the following information to create citations with a generator or to complete them yourself (information for websites and print sources differ slightly):

▶ Author(s)

▶ Publication title and type of publication: newspaper, book, website, etc.

▶ Publisher

▶ Date of publication

▶ Page numbers, especially if there are multiple pages, you are quoting directly from the publication, or you are using specific rather than general information

Create Your "Works Cited" List

▶ List all of the sources you have used in your essay on the Works Cited list at the end.

▶ Always list the author with the last name first. Then arrange the list by alphabetical order of the first word in each entry (usually the author's last name).

▶ Check with your teacher to see if he or she would like the actual Web address (URL) for an Internet source to appear in the citation. (The MLA no longer requires it.)

▶ Use these guidelines to create your Works Cited list for the sources on pages 54–57:

- **Magazine or Newspaper:** Author(s). "Title of Article." *Title of Periodical* Day Month Year: pages. Medium of publication.

- **Website:** Editor, author, or compiler name (if available). *Name of Site*. Version number. Name of institution/organization affiliated with the site (sponsor or publisher), date of resource creation (if available). Medium of publication. Date of access.

- **Book:** Author(s). *Title of Book*. Ed. Editor's Name. City of Publication: Publisher, Year. Page range of entry. Medium of publication.

© Houghton Mifflin Harcourt Publishing Company

Draft Your Essay

As you write, think about:

▶ **Audience:** Your teacher and your classmates

▶ **Purpose:** Demonstrate your understanding of the specific requirements of an informative essay.

▶ **Style:** Use a formal and objective tone.

▶ **Transitions:** Use words and phrases such as *on the other hand, likewise, on the contrary,* or *similarly* to create cohesion, or flow.

Check and Add Transitions

Transitions play a crucial role in making an essay read smoothly and in communicating your meaning. The primary roles of transitional words and phrases are to:

▶ introduce new paragraphs

▶ reveal the relationship between ideas within a paragraph

The lists of transitions in the chart are organized by what they can help you communicate. As you plan, write, and revise your essay, pay attention to how transitions can help you communicate clearly to your readers. **Tip:** Reading a paragraph from your essay aloud can help you "hear" where you have left out transitions that could help your ideas make sense.

Sequence or Chronological Order	Cause and Effect	Compare/ Contrast	Illustrating	Summarizing
• first, second, last • before, after • recently, in the past • initially, finally	• because, due to, on account of, this led to • as a result, one effect was, for this reason, this led to	• also, as well as, just as important, in a similar way • although, despite, in contrast, instead, on the other hand	• for example, this is shown by, in this case	• in the end, in general, overall, taken together

Review and Add Text Features

Text features can help make your meaning clear and help gain or hold a reader's attention. They should only be used if they relate to your central idea and add information or make reading the essay easier.

▶ **Titles** are important text features because if they are chosen carefully, they immediately tell the reader something about the subject of the essay.

▶ **Graphics,** such as photos, illustrations, charts, timelines, and maps can be drawn from the Internet, charts of information, or an annotated illustration. Be sure to credit the sources.

▶ **Subject headings or breaks** indicate what will follow or a change from one subject to another, such as a title and sub-headings.

▶ **Special vocabulary definitions** clarify words that will be unfamiliar to readers.

Revise

Revision Checklist: Self Evaluation

Use the checklist below to guide your analysis.

 If you drafted your essay on the computer, you may wish to print it out so that you can more easily evaluate it.

Ask Yourself	Tips	Revision Strategies
1. Does the introduction grab the audience's attention?	Underline sentences in the introduction that engage readers.	Add an interesting question, fact, or observation to get the reader's attention.
2. Are central ideas supported by evidence, facts, and details?	Circle evidence.	Add evidence if necessary.
3. Are appropriate and varied transitions used to explain ideas?	Place a checkmark next to each transitional word or phrase.	Add transitional words or phrases where needed to clarify the relationships between ideas.
4. Does the concluding section follow and sum up ideas? Does it give the audience something to think about?	Double underline the summary of key points in the concluding section. Underline the insight offered to readers.	Add an overarching view of key points or a final observation about the central idea and supporting details.
5. Are text features used that help clarify meaning or add interest?	Place rectangles around all text features.	Add one or more appropriate features only if they relate directly to the central idea and add information or simplify reading.
6. Are in-text citations and the Works Cited list used correctly?	Highlight in-text citations and review the Works Cited list.	Check that all information and facts cited in the text appear in a Works Cited list.

Revision Checklist: Peer Review

Exchange your essay with a classmate, or read it aloud to your partner. As you read and comment on your classmate's essay, focus on how clearly deep-sea creatures have been described. Help each other identify parts of the drafts that need strengthening, reworking, or even a completely new approach.

What To Look For	Notes for My Partner
1. Does the introduction grab the audience's attention?	
2. Is each central idea supported by evidence, facts, and concrete details?	
3. Are appropriate and varied transitions used to explain ideas?	
4. Does the concluding section follow and sum up ideas? Does it give the audience something to think about?	
5. Are text features (graphics, headings, vocabulary) used? Do they add information to the central idea or simplify reading?	
6. Are all facts and important information cited within the text? Is the Works Cited list complete and correctly formatted?	

Edit

 Edit your essay to correct spelling, grammar, and punctuation errors.

NOTES

How have Australian animals adapted to their environment?

You will read:

▶ **TWO INFORMATIVE ESSAYS**
   Australian Fauna

   New to Australia

You will write:

▶ **AN INFORMATIVE ESSAY**
   How have animals in Australia adapted to their environment?

Part 1: Read Sources

Source 1: Informative Essay

Australian Fauna
by Deirdre Manning

From *All about Australia*. International Travel Inc., undated, Web. Retrieved Sept. 22, 2014.

AS YOU READ *Identify key terms and ideas to use in your essay. For example, "marsupial" is a likely term to be used in both sources.*

NOTES

Early in geological history, Australia was cut off from the rest of the world's landmasses. This allowed a range of animals to establish successful populations in Australia—animals that were unable to do so in other parts of the world. In some cases, this separation meant that animals on Australia did not have natural predators, so they were able to thrive for thousands of years without competition. At the same time, the hot and dry climate in much of Australia forced animals to adapt to the environment so they could survive.

Separated from other land by miles of ocean, Australia is home to some unique types of animals. Most of Australia's native mammals are marsupials. Marsupials give birth to their young and then carry them in a pouch near their belly until the infant is old enough to survive on its own. Marsupials include kangaroos, wombats, Tasmanian devils, and koalas. Although marsupials didn't start in Australia (and some marsupials still exist in other places, such as South America), they have flourished there. They are well adapted to Australia because marsupials can survive using less energy than placental mammals so that over the millions of years in which Australia's climate became drier, they were able to get enough food from the grasses that took over the vegetation.

Another unusual type of Australian mammal is the monotreme. Monotremes lay eggs instead of giving birth to live young. There are only two types of monotremes in the world—the platypus and the echidna—and both of them are found in Australia. Monotremes require even less energy than marsupials. These animals have done very well in the harsh Australian climate.

Platypuses: Duck-like Feet and Bills

Platypuses are monotremes found all along the eastern coast of Australia, from Tasmania to far north Queensland. They are small dark-brown furry mammals

30 with webbed paws and duck-like beaks. Early observers suggested that a platypus had a duck's bill sewn on to a furry body.

A platypus

Platypuses live in burrows that they dig into the banks of rivers. This helps keep them cool in Australia's extreme heat. They are able to dig the burrows with their claws because when they are out of the water,

40 the webbing on their feet retracts so the claws are more prominent. They are diving animals, and can stay under water for up to two minutes. They have thick fur that keeps them warm underwater. Unlike a duck's beak, the platypus' beak is rubbery and flexible. It has hundreds of electroreceptor cells inside it, which can detect the electrical currents that are caused by its prey swimming through the water. This helps them hunt in murky water.

The diet of the platypus consists of worms, insects, shellfish, and larvae. A platypus will use its bill to find food in the mud and water. It also scoops up bits of gravel that help it mash up the food since it

50 actually doesn't have any teeth.

Platypuses give birth by laying eggs. The eggs are incubated by the mother in special nesting burrows. When it hatches, the baby platypus feeds on milk secreted from two patches of skin midway along the mother's belly.

Platypuses may look odd and harmless, but they are one of the only surviving mammals that use venom to protect themselves. Males have a small spur on their hind legs that can be used to against an attacker. The venom released isn't usually fatal, but it can cause permanent muscle damage to an unsuspecting attacker.

60 It is clear that the various physical attributes of the platypus, in addition to its lower energy requirements, have made it possible for the species to survive and thrive in Australia's difficult climate.

Echidnas: Spiny Anteaters

Echidnas can be found all over Australia. They also live in cool burrows as protection from the heat, although some subspecies have

adapted and grown denser fur to survive cold temperatures. They are small, round animals with large clawed feet, a long snout and a coat covered in sharp, flexible

70 spines. Their diet consists almost exclusively of termites, which is why they are also known as spiny anteaters. The long claws of the echidna are efficient at damaging termite mounds in order to get at the insects.

Echidnas have protective spines.

Like the platypus, echidnas also lay eggs. A female echidna lays a single egg that hatches in about ten days. The mother echidna carefully protects the baby echidna (or puggle) until it begins to develop spines.

80 The echidna's spines are used mainly as a defense mechanism. They are strong and sharp and provide defense against predators such as dingoes. However, Tasmanian devils will eat echidnas—even the spines. When threatened, an echidna will either roll itself into a spiky ball or dig itself into the ground until only its spines are exposed.

Emus: Birds that Don't Fly

Although they aren't related to the monotremes or marsupials, emus are another of the unique animals found in Australia. They are large, flightless birds with hairy, brown feathers that they can fluff up to stay warm in colder weather. Standing up to six feet tall and

90 weighing an average of 60 kilograms, emus are the second largest bird in the world and have long necks that help them reach food. Their eyes are also interesting because they have a clear membrane that protects their eyes by keeping them moist and preventing dust from getting in. Emus can be found all over Australia, away from settled areas.

Emus have a stride that measures around nine feet and can run at speeds of up to 50 kilometres per hour. This speed is useful in avoiding predators such as dingoes, particularly since Emus can't fly. They travel large distances in pairs or small groups, though

100 occasionally large herds of up to a thousand have been formed.

1. Analyze   2. Practice   3. Perform

Emus have fairly large territories and can travel up to 900 kilometres in a nine-month period. If there is a reliable source of water, emus will stay nearby. They mainly tend to travel long distances in search of water. Their diet consists of leaves, grasses, fruits, native plants, and insects. Emu young are called chicks.

Kangaroos: A Symbol of Australia

The marsupials of Australia are known around the world. The kangaroo is often seen as a symbol of Australia. It is Australia's largest marsupial and is unique because it travels by hopping on long hind legs. Scientists aren't sure why this trait developed since it not

110 an efficient way to travel except at top speeds. However, kangaroos can reach speeds of up to 56 kilometres per hour and can jump distances of eight metres and heights of almost two metres, abilities that make it easier for them to escape any predators. Another trait that is helpful is a kangaroo's ability to swivel its ears to hear sounds from different directions. This helps a kangaroo notice predators.

Kangaroos live in large packs (or mobs) of around 100. Their diet consists of grasses, leaves, and other plants. In the dry areas of Australia, they thrive wherever a regular water source is available. The introduction of European farming methods has established

120 regular water supplies and allowed the kangaroo population to grow dramatically. It is estimated that there are around twenty million kangaroos in Australia. Modern kangaroos developed teeth that are good for grazing on grasses in dry climates, an adaptation that allowed it to do well as the climate of Australia changed.

A baby kangaroo is called a joey. Joeys are raised in their mother's pouch, suckling from the teats inside, until they are about ten months old. Within a few days of giving birth, female kangaroos enter into heat and will mate again and, if they successfully conceive, after one week's development the microscopic embryo enters a

130 dormant state that will last until the previous young leaves the pouch. The second embryo then resumes development and proceeds to birth after a gestation period of about 30 days.

Discuss and Decide

What are some attributes of platypuses, echidnas, and kangaroos that help them survive the Australian environment? Cite textual evidence in your response.

Wombats: Grazing at Night

The wombat is the world's largest burrowing herbivorous mammal. They average one meter in length and 25–35 centimeters in height. Wombats have four powerful legs that they use for digging, and large heads with small eyes, pointed ears, and prominent snouts. Wombats are found mainly on the east coast of Australia, from Tasmania to southern Queensland.

Wombats are nocturnal animals. Nocturnal animals are active by night and sleep during the day. During summer, wombats spend almost eighty per cent of their time underground. This adaptation to nighttime activity allows it to stay cool in its long, complex burrow during the day. They mainly leave their burrows at night when the air temperature is cooler, but in colder weather they can be seen out during the day as well.

Wombats are grazing animals, eating mainly grass and other plants, including shrubs, roots, bark and moss. When feeding, a wombat can pick up its food with one of its front feet and place it straight into its mouth. Wombat young are called joeys and the female wombat has a pouch that faces backwards. This attribute is an adaptation that prevents dirt from entering the pouch when the wombat is burrowing.

Tasmanian Devils: Meat Eaters with Bad Tempers

The Tasmanian devil is the world's largest carnivorous marsupial. It is roughly the size of a dog, and is thick-set with a muscular build, a large, wide head and a short, thick tail. The devil's fur is black and usually has patches of white on its chest and rump. People who saw them during the day named them devils because of they often snarled and showed their teeth.

This Tasmanian devil doesn't look fearsome, but it can scare off an intruder with a snarl.

Tasmanian devils are only found in Tasmania, though fossil evidence shows that there were devils on the Australian mainland 3,500 years ago. Tasmanian devils have powerful jaws

140

150

160

1. Analyze   2. Practice   3. Perform

170 and long, sharp teeth. They are primarily nocturnal, coming out at night. This adaptation allows them to take advantage of cooler temperatures to forage for food. Devils are scavengers, sometimes eating small mammals as prey, but mainly living on the remains of dead animals. When feeding, a Tasmanian devil has strong jaws and teeth that allow it to eat everything, including bones and fur. The ability of the Tasmanian devil to consume many different things that other animals might not eat allows it to survive where sources of food may not be plentiful.

Generally speaking Tasmanian devils are solitary animals, but packs
180 of devils will feed communally on larger dead animals they find, like cattle and sheep.

Koalas: Cuddly Little Bears

Koalas are tree-dwelling marsupials whose diet consists almost exclusively of the leaves of a particular type of tree called Eucalyptus. Koalas have grey fur similar to sheep's wool, large prominent ears and a round face. Their limbs are long and muscular and their paws are broad with long claws. They can be found throughout mainland eastern Australia.

Koalas' paws have rough pads and long claws that are adapted to help them climb Eucalyptus trees to find food. A koala's front paw
190 has three fingers and two opposing digits, almost like two separate thumbs. The hind paws have a clawless opposing digit and two toes that are fused together to form a "grooming claw."

Koalas spend twenty hours a day sleeping or resting. The rest of the time is spent feeding, grooming and moving from tree to tree. The koalas' diet of eucalyptus leaves is a very low-energy diet, which accounts for their low levels of activity. However, koala's ability to survive on a low-energy food source has helped them be successful in the difficult Australian environment. In the dry Australian climate, their main source of water is the dew and rain that collects on the
200 leaves they eat. Koala young are called joeys.

Discuss and Decide

How has the ability to survive on a low-energy diet and/or eat less desirable food sources helped some Australian animals? Explain using text evidence.

Source 2: Informative Essay

NEW TO AUSTRALIA

by Aidan Semmler in *Queensland Habitat Journal,* May 18, 2013

AS YOU READ *Identify topics addressed in this article that were addressed in the previous source.*

NOTES

Unique to Australia

More than 80 percent of the plants, mammals, reptiles, and frogs found in Australia are not found anywhere else in the world. The only placental mammals (all mammals that are not marsupials or monotremes) native to Australia are the house mouse and some species of rats and bats. This is not to say that there are only these few species of placental mammals in Australia; rabbits, foxes, and even camels are common, but they were introduced species. Australia had developed an ecology that was unique due to its remoteness. Once settlers arrived, they brought with them familiar 10 animals, along with unexpected consequences.

How Introduced Species are Successful and Damaging

The story of **rabbits** in Australia is a remarkable one. In 1859, a settler named Thomas Austin released 24 rabbits so that he could continue the hunting that he had enjoyed in England. Within ten years there were so many rabbits loose in Australia that even though about two million were shot or trapped each year, it didn't make a dent in their population. Over time, the rabbits have caused untold damage to Australia's native plants and animals. Destroying the plants has left less food for other animals and also causes erosion. The topsoil gets washed away and the land can no longer support 20 vegetation. Rabbits are thought to have caused more species loss in Australia than any other other cause.

Close Read

Explain what the author means by "introduced species." Cite textual evidence in your response.

_____

1. Analyze   2. Practice   3. Perform

Like rabbits, **foxes** were introduced in Australia for hunting. They were originally brought over in the mid-1800s. There are now more than seven million red foxes in Australia. They are a successful predator, responsible for the decline or extinction of many native species.

Other introduced mammals that cause damage include over a million feral camels, two million feral goats, twenty million feral pigs, and eighteen million feral cats. The word *feral* refers to animals
30 that are living in the wild but are descended from domesticated animals. These animals have lived in Australia for hundreds of years now, and have very few predators. This accounts for their huge successes as species, resulting in the major damage they inflict on the Australian ecosystem.

Perhaps most surprisingly dangerous to Australian ecology is a humble toad. The **cane toad** was introduced from Hawaii in 1935 to try to combat the native cane beetle, which was destroying much of the sugar cane crop. The cane toad population has now topped 200 million, causing major environmental damage. The toads are toxic,
40 and native predators have no immunity to the poison. Toads can kill native predators such as the quoll, a cat-like marsupial that is also hunted by the red fox. The cane toad does not seem to have had any effect on the cane beetle: The cane beetles moved too high on the cane stalks for the cane toads to reach.

Encourage Dingoes to Help Other Species?

Bearing in mind the havoc caused by species introduction, it is remarkable that people are suggesting the reintroduction on a large scale of another non-native species. The **dingo** is a wild dog that appears to have reached Australia about 4,000 years ago. It is believed that dingoes are descended from domesticated dogs and
50 were brought by seafaring people from Asia. The dingo is now Australia's largest carnivorous mammal. (That position used to belong to the Tasmanian tiger, a marsupial mammal that is now extinct. Tasmanian tigers were hunted enthusiastically in the nineteenth century, and the last of the species died in a zoo in 1936.) Most people regard the dingo as a true Australian because of its long residence down under. It is suggested that scarcity of dingoes allowed smaller, non-native, predators to hunt and cause the extinction of many native marsupials. Encouraging a larger population of dingoes to hunt these predators (and animals such as rabbits) might result in
60 better conditions for native marsupials, which could flourish more easily than in an ecosystem in which introduced species either prey on them or devour their food.

Part 2: Write

Plan

Use the graphic organizer to help you outline the structure of your informative essay. Remember to use another sheet of paper to add additional points or subjects to your essay if necessary.

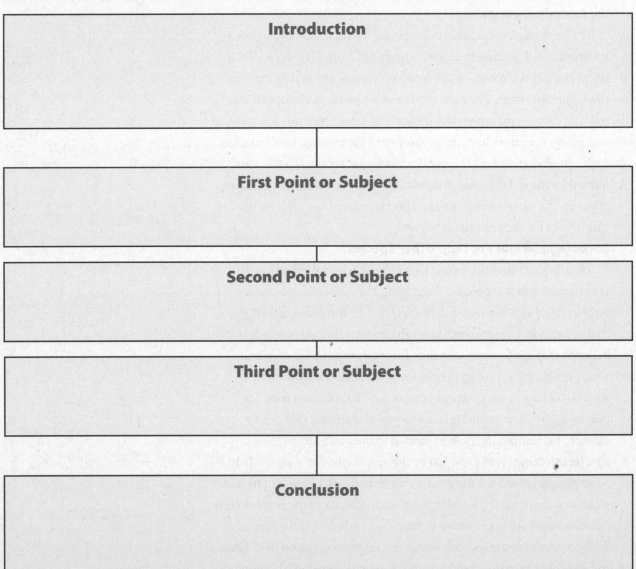

Introduction

First Point or Subject

Second Point or Subject

Third Point or Subject

Conclusion

Draft

 Use your notes and completed graphic organizer to write a first draft of your essay.

Revise and Edit

 Look back over your essay and compare it to the Evaluation Criteria. Revise your essay and edit it to correct spelling, grammar, and punctuation errors.

Evaluation Criteria

Your teacher will be looking for:

1. *Statement of purpose*

▶ Did you support your points with evidence?

2. *Organization*

▶ Are the sections of your essay organized in a logical way?

▶ Is there a smooth flow from beginning to end?

▶ Is there a clear conclusion that supports the comparisons?

▶ Did you stay on topic?

3. *Elaboration of evidence*

▶ Is the evidence relevant to the topic?

▶ Is there enough evidence?

4. *Conventions*

▶ Did you follow the rules of grammar usage as well as punctuation, capitalization, and spelling?

▶ Did you cite all your sources, both in the text of your essay and in a Works Cited list, using the correct MLA formats?

NOTES

Inspirations

UNIT 3

Literary Analysis

STEP

1

ANALYZE THE MODEL

Evaluate a student model about how William Stafford's experiences and ideas are reflected in his poem "Fifteen."

STEP

2

PRACTICE THE TASK

Write an essay that explores connections between Walt Whitman's life experiences and his writing, based on several prose works and a poem by Whitman.

STEP

3

PERFORM THE TASK

Write an essay that explores the ways in which Elizabeth Barrett Browning's life experiences influenced her poetry.

What inspires you? The word *inspiration* comes from the Latin word *spirare*, meaning "to breathe," and has the same root as the word *spirit*. We humans need inspiration almost as much as we need air to breathe. Fortunately, life provides many sources of inspiration. The experiences of everyday life can inspire us to set new goals and take meaningful action. Writers, inspired by the full range of life's experiences, weave their observations and feelings into poems, stories, essays, letters, and other literary works.

Why would someone write a poem about a motorcyle accident that focuses on the thoughts and feelings of a teenage observer? Readers may gain insight into William Stafford's poem "Fifteen" by learning more about the poet's biography and his attitude toward life. Similarly, taking a broader view of Walt Whitman's life experiences can help readers analyze his poetry and prose writing.

Elizabeth Barrett Browning wrote the memorable words "How do I love thee? Let me count the ways." Her real-life love story with her husband, Robert Browning, provided the emotional fuel for her romantic poetry.

IN THIS UNIT, you will analyze one student's response to the poem "Fifteen" by William Stafford. Then, you will read several works by Walt Whitman and analyze how his life experiences are reflected in his writing. Finally, you will analyze how Elizabeth Barrett Browning's life influenced her "Sonnet 43," based on biographical information and personal letters.

© Houghton Mifflin Harcourt Publishing Company

ANALYZE THE MODEL

What makes an experience important?

You will read:

▶ **A BIOGRAPHY**
William Stafford: The Poet and His Craft

▶ **AN ESSAY**
"What Is a Current Event?"

▶ **A POEM**
"Fifteen"

You will analyze:

▶ **A STUDENT MODEL**
Life and Art: William Stafford's "Fifteen"

Source Materials for Step 1

Mr. Lewis assigned the following biography, essay, and poem to his class to read and analyze. The notes in the side columns were written by Jennifer Ricardo, a student in Mr. Lewis's class.

William Stafford: The Poet and His Craft
by Aleesha Berwick

Poet William Stafford (1914–1993) was born in Hutchinson, Kansas. Stafford was the oldest of three children in a family with a great love for literature. During the Great Depression, his family moved from town to town seeking work. Stafford contributed to the family's income by delivering newspapers, working in sugar-beet fields, raising vegetables, and working as an electrician's apprentice.

Stafford was a conscientious objector who refused to take up arms during World War II. Instead, he worked in the civilian public service camps. He later wrote a fictionalized memoir of that time called *Down in My Heart* (1947). His first major collection of poetry, *Traveling Through the Dark* (1962), was published when he was forty-eight years old. It won the National Book Award. He went on to publish more than sixty-five volumes of poetry and prose.

Western landscapes were the backdrop of Stafford's life—and his writing. He described the homes of his youth as being on the outskirts of town, on the cusp of "adventure, fields forever, or rivers that wended off over the horizon, forever. And in the center of town was a library, another kind of edge out there forever, to explore." Critics have noted that many of his poems describe open spaces stretching into the distance, inviting exploration.

Stafford's poems can be deceptively simple—written in familiar language but focused on complex feelings and ideas. He once remarked that the voice he heard in his poems was that of his mother, who had "an attitude of not being impressed by the sort of stance or posture that most people take." In his writing, he imagined himself "communicating with a peer" rather than talking up—or down—to the reader. His quiet, conversational style conveys meaning in an understated way.

Posted June 8, 2014, at *Poets We Love* (Words Matter, LLC).

That's pretty late to start writing poetry!

I like the idea of exploring different kinds of horizons— physical, literary, and maybe others.

Interesting how his mother's no-nonsense voice stayed in his head. I'll listen for this voice in his poem.

1. Analyze   2. Practice   3. Perform

What Is a Current Event?
by William Stafford

It's true—some of what we read in school seems disconnected from real life.

This is a different way to define "current events"— not big news stories, but what's happening to me right now.

News accounts of the Korean War didn't mention all the personal stories that made up the big story.

Big events have an impact on the small details of people's lives, and vice versa.

More and more in literature class the students listen less and less to the books; the books are about something that has already happened, or that didn't happen at all. Whereas all good students know that real events, current events, important events are happening every day, outside there, away from literature. It is like a big bass drum beating outside the window. Who can study against that throb?

And yet, the trouble with those big events is that they happen to other people; how about the current events that happen to us—to you and me? Inside here, away from the bass drum, current events happen; and the drum cannot become loud enough to drown out the important events inside, the really current, really important, events.

This morning an army of a million men crossed the thirty-eighth parallel in Korea. That's a current event, but only in terms of the real little events that compose it. One soldier was walking along on the dusty road carrying a pack that was too heavy and that had a knob that dug into his back. He hadn't been able to eat breakfast; he was thinking about how the road ahead looked like the road out north of the home town. When he stopped to adjust his pack an enemy rifleman, a hungry, cold man lost from his group, raised his gun, sighted over the smudgy barrel, and shot the soldier. That is a current event.

At the time of the crossing a diplomat in a neutral country was drinking his coffee. He put down his napkin and answered the phone. Now he would have to hurry to the consulate, prepare a report, stop by to pick up the groceries, put out of his mind the thought of helping his son with his schoolwork. The diplomat's coffee was cold when he put down the receiver. That's a current event.

In the house of the commanding general the room was cold. He had to leave the telephone to go call for more fuel; during his absence the phone rang for advice, but the reply was delayed; one sector of the front delayed too long; the wave of advance was over; hundreds of men died. And the general found the orderly, who found the oil for the stove, which heated the room. That is a current event.

In our room one student read the story for today and saw in it something that changed his life. That story, the reading of it, was a current event. The bass drum was beating outside.

The front line was stabilized again; the enemy commander had gone out for fuel too; his troops waited too long and a mountain pass filled with snow. The lines settled back to where they were before. Millions of people experienced millions of events, all of them current. The editor beat the drum for certain events; hearts beat for others. And the experiences that make events, they are where you find them—and most of them not in the sound of the drum.

From *Crossing Unmarked Snow* (Ann Arbor: The University of Michigan Press, 1998), pages 155–156.

Stafford believes literature itself can be a current event, because it has an immediate impact on the reader.

Discuss and Decide

Based on this essay, what might you expect Stafford's poetry to be like? Discuss your ideas with a partner, citing evidence from the essay.

▼

1. Analyze   2. Practice   3. Perform

Fifteen

by William Stafford

South of the bridge on Seventeenth
I found back of the willows one summer
day a motorcycle with engine running
as it lay on its side, ticking over
5   slowly in the high grass. I was fifteen.

I admired all that pulsing gleam, the
shiny flanks, the demure headlights
fringed where it lay; I led it gently
to the road and stood with that
10 companion, ready and friendly. I was fifteen.

We could find the end of a road, meet
the sky on out Seventeenth. I thought about
hills, and patting the handle got back a
confident opinion. On the bridge we indulged
15 a forward feeling, a tremble. I was fifteen.

Thinking, back farther in the grass I found
the owner, just coming to, where he had flipped
over the rail. He had blood on his hand, was pale—
I helped him walk to his machine. He ran his hand
20 over it, called me good man, roared away.

I stood there, fifteen.

This phrase in line 2 sounds like ordinary conversation.

"Demure" usually describes a person, not a machine.

Motorcycle is like a horse—or a love interest.

Here is one of those wide-open spaces!

Did the speaker ride the motorcycle or not?

From *The Way It Is: New and Selected Poems*
(Saint Paul, MN: Graywolf Press, 1998),
page 201.

Discuss and Decide

What words in the last stanza signal a shift in the speaker's view? What does the speaker realize at this point?

Analyze a Student Model for Step 1

Read Jennifer's literary analysis closely. The red side notes are the comments that her teacher, Mr. Lewis, wrote.

Jennifer Ricardo
Mr. Lewis, English
April 24

Life and Art:
William Stafford's "Fifteen"

William Stafford's poem "Fifteen" tells a simple story. One summer, a teenage boy finds a motorcycle by the side of the road and fantasizes about riding it. He then locates its owner, who has had an accident and fallen. The boy returns the bike to him.

Your second paragraph outlines the topics you will discuss in the essay. This makes your organization clear to readers.

However, there is much more happening in the poem than just this simple encounter. When we analyze it carefully, we also find the poet's life experiences and philosophy reflected in many of its details, including the setting, voice, and point of view. Knowing about the author's biography and his perspective on life helps us analyze his writing on a deeper level and understand it more fully.

Stafford was born in Kansas and spent much of his life surrounded by Western landscapes. Recalling his childhood, he said that he looked out from the edges of the towns where his family lived to see "adventure, fields forever, or rivers that wended off over the horizon, forever" (Berwick). These kinds of wide-open spaces that call out to be explored appear in many of his poems. In "Fifteen," the speaker imagines that he and the motorcycle could "find the end of a road, meet / the sky out on Seventeenth" (11–12). For this teenage boy, the horizon symbolizes adulthood, which he is eager to experience.

I like the way you've incorporated a quotation from the biography and connected it to specific lines in the poem.

The voice of the poem is conversational. The speaker wishes to share his memory with readers, to tell them a good story and help them relate to his feelings. Stafford once said that the voice he heard in his poems was that of his mother, who loved to read but had no patience for literary posturing (Berwick). The speaker in "Fifteen" uses expressions such as "back of the willows" and "just coming to" that sound like ordinary conversation (2, 17).

The poem's point of view is interesting when we consider what a newspaper account of the events would say. The news story would focus on the motorcycle accident and what happened to the adult rider. If the boy were mentioned at all, it would be to say that he helped the man to his feet. However, Stafford believed that big news events are actually made up of small events that affect individual lives ("What Is a Current Event?" 155–156). It is not surprising that he chooses to tell this story from the point of view of someone who has an intense emotional reaction to finding the motorcycle and dreaming about riding it. For the fifteen-year-old speaker, his yearnings and anxieties about adulthood are the main event.

"Fifteen" is worth reading simply for its insights into the emotions of a teenage boy. However, knowing more about the writer's background and ideas allows the reader to get much more meaning from the poem. Its setting on the edge of a wide-open space evokes Stafford's attitude toward life's exciting possibilities. The way it is told from the point of view of someone on the margins of the "real" action—the motorcycle accident—and its conversational voice reflect Stafford's belief that the everyday events that happen to ordinary people are just as important as the headline news. In fact, those small events are the essential building blocks without which the big events could not exist.

Good examples of conversational language.

Interesting point about what kinds of events make the news versus what is important to individuals.

Your conclusion is strong. You provide a good summary of the interaction between the poet's life and his work. Nice job!

Works Cited

Berwick, Aleesha. "William Stafford: The Poet and His Craft." *Poets We Love.* Words Matter, LLC, 8 June 2014. Web. 13 Apr. 2015.

Stafford, William. "Fifteen." *The Way It Is: New and Selected Poems.* Saint Paul, MN: Graywolf Press, 1998. 201. Print.

---. "What Is a Current Event?" *Crossing Unmarked Snow.* Ann Arbor: The University of Michigan Press, 1998. 155–156. Print.

Discuss and Decide

How did Jennifer use the biography and the essay to inform her analysis of the poem? Cite text evidence in your discussion.

NOTES

How can real events inspire poetry and other writing?

You will read:

▶ **AN ESSAY**
Taking a Biographical Approach to Literary Criticism

▶ **A BIOGRAPHY**
Walt Whitman

▶ **A NEWSPAPER ARTICLE**
from *"Letters from Paumanok"*

▶ **A POEM**
"I Hear America Singing"

▶ **A JOURNAL ENTRY**
"The Real War Will Never Get in the Books"

▶ **A LETTER**
"Letter to His Mother"

You will write:

▶ **A LITERARY ANALYSIS**
Analyze how Whitman's life experiences are reflected in his writing.

Source Materials for Step 2

AS YOU READ You will be writing a literary analysis that explores how Whitman's life experiences are reflected in his poem "I Hear America Singing" and his journal entry "The Real War Will Never Get in the Books." As you read about Whitman's life and work, underline and circle information that may be useful to you when you write your essay.

Source 1: Essay

Taking a Biographical Approach to Literary Criticism

by Kylene Beers, posted January 7, 2013, at *Deep Reading* website

Read this conversation that I once had with a group of high school students. See if you've ever had a reaction like Adam's.

> "So, what do you think about the story?" I asked.
> "I liked it," some said. Others just nodded. Some just sat.
> "Well, what can you tell me about the author from reading this story?" I asked.
> Silence for a while and finally Adam said, "I didn't read anything about the author. I just read the story."

Adam was right—he did just read the story—but he was also wrong. When reading a story or a poem, you can sometimes make inferences, or guesses, about its writer. Consider this situation: You read a story about a character who suffers through a tough experience, but in the end is celebrated for her bravery. You can guess that the author believes that bravery should be rewarded.

You can't always presume, however, that a writer has had the same experiences that he or she writes about. For example, you can't presume that a writer lived through the events he or she describes in a short story about a high school athlete, even though the writer might have been a high school athlete herself. You can conclude, however, that the writer understands what it is *like* to compete in high school athletics.

Sometimes, however, a writer does use a personal experience or an actual event in a short story or poem. For example, Walt Whitman wrote many poems and articles about the Civil War. He knew about this topic and felt strongly about it in part because he had spent time working as a nurse in the war, witnessing its devastating effects on people. When you take a biographical approach to literary criticism, you think about an author's life experiences as you respond to and analyze the text as a reader.

[handwritten note:] You shouldn't guess what the author went through— it might be wrong

[handwritten note:] Walt Whitman was a nurse during a war

Source 2: Biography

Walt Whitman

by Mark Botha

One of nine children, Walt Whitman (1819–1892) grew up in Brooklyn, New York, and Long Island and experienced both the community of country life and the urban bustle of a growing new city. As a young man, he plied many trades, including printer, teacher, and journalist. By the time he was twenty, his fascination with the boomtown atmosphere of Brooklyn led him to journalism. After ten years of reporting, he took a kind of working vacation—a difficult overland journey to New Orleans. He put his journalistic talent to work at the New Orleans *Crescent* while also observing the alien culture of New Orleans and the brutal face of slavery that existed there.

Returning to Brooklyn, Whitman served as editor of the *Brooklyn Freeman* while supplementing his income as a part-time carpenter and contractor. He also wrote for other newspapers, including a series in the *New York Evening Post* in 1851 called "Letters from Paumanok." He signed each letter with the pseudonym *Paumanok,* the Lenape name for Long Island. The articles show his experimentation with a first-person style of journalism that brings the reader along as Whitman explores neighborhoods and interacts with ordinary people. During this period, Whitman kept notebooks and began assembling the sprawling collection of poems that would transform his life and change the course of American literature.

[Handwritten annotations:]
- grew up in many different cities
- Whitman was many things
- Stopped writing to see the brutal slaves that were there.
- Kept his writing to himself (to save) and then might make it public

In 1855, Whitman self-published his groundbreaking collection of poetry, *Leaves of Grass*. Its original style drew lifelong admirers, including Ralph Waldo Emerson, and many critics, who condemned it as "disreputable." *Leaves of Grass* was expanded and revised through many editions until the ninth "deathbed" edition was published in 1892, thirty-seven years after its first appearance. It is a spiritual autobiography that tells the story of an enchanted observer who says how he is inspired at every opportunity.

When Whitman learned that his younger brother had been wounded in Fredericksburg, Virginia, he immediately traveled to the front. There he saw the aftermath of one of the war's bloodiest battles. This experience convinced him to work in Washington, D.C., as a volunteer nurse. While caring for the wounded, Whitman witnessed the effects of war on men's bodies and minds. During this time, he wrote numerous poems. His years of nursing, he once wrote, were "the greatest privilege and satisfaction . . . and, of course, the most profound lesson of my life."

Beset by ill-health, Whitman suffered a stroke in 1873. However, his influence continued to grow as he released new editions of *Leaves of Grass*. In the preface to one of these editions, Whitman wrote: "The proof of a poet is that his country absorbs him as affectionately as he has absorbed it." He believed there was a vital relationship between the poet and society. Whitman died on March 26, 1892. His funeral drew thousands of mourners, and his casket could not even be seen for the many wreaths of flowers left upon it.

Posted September 27, 2014, at *World Wide Poetry Blog* (World Wide Poetry, Inc.).

Discuss and Decide

Why might Whitman have called his experiences nursing in the Civil War "the most profound lesson" of his life? What do you think he learned?

1. Analyze   2. Practice   3. Perform

Source 3: Newspaper Article

Background: *In this article, Whitman describes walking around a village on Long Island with a friend. Along the way, he meets an old man wearing "a truly wonderful hat." Later, Whitman stops on a bridge and sees the man again, digging for clams.*

from *Letters from Paumanok*
by Walt Whitman

A couple of rods from the shore, and near at hand, was the old gentleman, with the remarkable hat; he had arrived before us, and was busily engaged with his hoe, digging a basket of soft clams, "for bait," as he said. He procured quite a mess in fifteen minutes, and then brought them up, and sat down on the bridge by me, to rest himself.

A Colloquy[1]—"Aunt Rebby"

Lighting his pipe very deliberately, he proceeded to catechise[2] me as to my name, birth-place, and lineage—where I was from last, where I was staying, what my occupation was, and so on. Having satisfied himself on these important points, I thought it no more than fair to return the compliment in kind, and so pitched into

10 him.[3]

He was born on the spot where he now lived; that very same Rocky Point. He was sixty-seven years old. For twenty years he had kept a butcher's stall in Fly Market, in New York, and left that business to move back on the "old homestead."

He volunteered the information that he was a Universalist in his religious belief, and asked my opinion upon the merits of the preachers of that faith, Mr. Chapin, Mr. Thayer, Mr. Balch, and others. He also commenced what he probably intended for a religious argument; and there was no other way than for me to stop him off, by direct inquiries into the state of his family and his real estate.

He was "well off" in both respects, possessing a farm of over a hundred acres,
20 running from the turnpike to the Sound,[4] and being the father of numerous sons and daughters. He expatiated on the merits of his land at great length; and was just going into those of his bodily offspring, when our confab[5] was fated to receive a sudden interruption. For at this moment came along an old woman with a little tin kettle in her hand.

---

[1] **colloquy:** conversation.
[2] **catechise:** ask questions of, interview.
[3] **pitched into him:** began asking him questions.
[4] **the Sound:** Long Island Sound, which separates Long Island from Bronx and Westchester counties, New York, and Connecticut.
[5] **confab:** confabulation, a casual chat.

[Handwritten annotations: "Asked the guy questions in return"; "Was a butcher for 20 years and left to come back home"; "He was lucky- had many children and owned a farm"; "Someone interrupted their conversation and a women came with a thin kettle"]

"Aunt Rebby," at once exclaimed the old gentleman, "don't you know me?"

But Aunt Rebby seemed oblivious.

"Is it possible you don't know me? Why we've bussed[6] one another many a time in our young days!"

A new light broke upon the dim eyes of the old dame.

30   "Why Uncle Dan'l!" cried she, "can this be you?"

Uncle Dan'l averred that it wasn't any body else. And then ensued a long gossip, of which I was the edified[7] and much-amused hearer. They had not met each other, it seems, for years, and there needed to be a long interchange of news.

"What a fine mess of clams you've got," said the old lady.

"Yes," responded Uncle Dan'l.

"But I," rejoined the old lady, in a mournful voice—"I have no body to dig clams for me now."

"No, I s'pose not," said the other, composedly; "your boys are all gone now."

Supposing that the "boys" had emigrated to California, or married and moved 40 off, I ventured an inquiry as to where they had gone.

Three young men, all the sons of the old woman, had died of consumption.[8] The last was buried only a short time before.

Old times were talked of. Aunt Rebby expressed it as her positive opinion that the young folks of the present day don't enjoy half as much fun as the young folks of fifty years ago, and a little longer, did. She was seventy years old, and remembered the days of General Washington. Those were jovial times, but now "it was all pride, fashion and ceremony."

From *The Uncollected Poetry and Prose of Walt Whitman*, edited by Emory Holloway (Garden City, NY: Doubleday, Page & Company, 1921), pages 252–253.

---

[6] **bussed:** met.

[7] **edified:** informed, educated.

[8] **consumption:** tuberculosis, an infectious disease of the lungs.

Discuss and Decide

What is Whitman's tone, or attitude, toward the man in the remarkable hat? Cite evidence for your response.

1. Analyze   2. Practice   3. Perform

Source 4: Poem

I Hear America Singing

by Walt Whitman

[handwritten annotation: care free happy feeling →]

I hear America singing, the varied carols I hear,

Those of mechanics, each one singing his as it should be <u>blithe</u> and
    strong,

The carpenter singing his as he measures his plank or beam,

[handwritten annotation: The carpenter is singing as he's doing his work]

The <u>mason</u> singing his as he makes ready for work, or leaves off
    work,

5 The <u>boatman</u> singing what belongs to him in his boat, the
    deckhand singing on the steamboat deck,

The <u>shoemaker</u> singing as he sits on his bench, the hatter singing as
    he stands,

The wood-cutter's song, the <u>ploughboy's</u> on his way in the morning,
    or at noon intermission or at sundown,

[handwritten annotation: Listed 9 people doing things — all have common: Singing + different jobs]

The delicious singing of the <u>mother</u>, or of the <u>young wife</u> at work,
    or of the <u>girl</u> sewing or washing,

[handwritten annotation: Everyone's singing belongs to themselves]

Each singing what belongs to him or her and to none else,

10 The day what belongs to the day—at night the party of young
    fellows, robust, friendly,

Singing with open mouths their strong melodious songs.

**From *Leaves of Grass* (Boston: Small, Maynard & Company,
1904), page 17.**

Close Read

How would you describe the speaker's tone toward American workers? Cite
evidence from the poem in your response.

_____

_____

_____

Source 5: Journal Entry

The Real War Will Never Get in the Books
by Walt Whitman

And so good-bye to the war. . . .

Future years will never know the seething hell and the black infernal
background of countless minor scenes and interiors, (not the official surface
courteousness of the Generals, not the few great battles) of the Secession[1] war; and
it is best they should not—the real war will never get in the books. In the mushy
influences of current times, too, the fervid[2] atmosphere and typical events of those
years are in danger of being totally forgotten. I have at night watch'd by the side of
a sick man in the hospital, one who could not live many hours. I have seen his eyes
flash and burn as he raised himself and recurr'd to the cruelties on his surrender'd
10 brother, and mutilations of the corpse afterward. . . .

The hospital part of the drama from '61 to '65, deserves indeed to be recorded.
Of that many-threaded drama, . . . the marrow of the tragedy concentrated in those
Army Hospitals—(it seem'd sometimes as if the whole interest of the land, North
and South, was one vast central hospital, and all the rest of the affair but flanges[3])—
those forming the untold and unwritten history of the war—infinitely greater
(like life's) than the few scraps and distortions that are ever told or written. Think
how much, and of importance, will be—how much, civic and military, has already
been—buried in the grave, in eternal darkness.

**From *The Complete Prose Works of Walt Whitman*, Vol. 1 (New York: G. P.
Putnam's Sons, 1902), pages 139–142.**

---

[1] **Secession:** the effort by Southern states to secede or withdraw from the United States in
the Civil War.
[2] **fervid:** passionate.
[3] **flanges:** external parts that strengthen or hold together an object in the center.

Handwritten margin notes:
- *Saying bye to war — meaning he won't see it happen again*
- *Witnessed an injured and sick man from the war*
- *The writers wouldn't write the truth about the war*
- *violence has been buried (gone)*

Discuss and Decide

According to Whitman, how is the recorded history of the war different from
the real war? Cite evidence for your response.

▼

96   1. Analyze   2. Practice   3. Perform

Source 6: Letter

Background: *In this letter to his mother, Whitman describes a meaningful encounter with a wounded Union soldier following the Battle of Fredericksburg.*

Letter to His Mother

by Walt Whitman

January 29, 1865

Dear Mother—

[handwritten: Talking about a wounded soldier]

Here is a case of a soldier I found among the crowded cots in the Patent hospital—(they have removed most of the men of late and broken up that hospital). He likes to have some one to talk to, and we will listen to him. He got badly wounded in the leg and side at Fredericksburg that eventful Saturday, 13th December. He lay the succeeding two days and nights helpless on the field, between the city and those grim batteries, for his company and his regiment had been compelled to leave him to his fate. To make matters worse, he lay with his head slightly down hill, and could not help himself.

10 At the end of some fifty hours he was brought off, with other wounded, under a flag of truce.

[handwritten: Asked the wounded guy some questions]

We ask him how the Rebels treated him during those two days and nights within reach of them—whether they came to him—whether they abused him? He answers that several of the Rebels, soldiers and others, came to him, at one time and another. A couple of them, who were together, spoke roughly and sarcastically, but did no act. One middle-aged man, however, who seemed to be moving around the field among the dead and wounded for benevolent

A man came and started to treat the wounded man better

purposes, came to him in a way he will never forget. This <u>man</u>
20 <u>treated our soldier kindly, bound up his wounds, cheered him,</u>
<u>gave him a couple of biscuits, gave him a drink and water, asked</u>
<u>him if he could eat some beef.</u> This good Secesh, however, did not
change our soldier's position, for it might have caused the blood
to burst from the wounds where they were clotted and stagnated.
Our soldier is from Pennsylvania; <u>has had a pretty severe time;</u> the
<u>wounds proved to be bad ones.</u> But he <u>retains a good heart, and is at</u>
<u>present on the gain</u>. . . .

The guy who was injured still had a good heart even tho he was wounded really badly.

Walt

**Posted May 31, 2009, at *Walt Whitman Online*
(Herba College).**

Discuss and Decide

Which lines of "Letter to His Mother" connect in some way with lines from "The
Real War Will Never Get in the Books"? Be sure to include specific lines in your
thinking and discussion.

1. Analyze   2. Practice   3. Perform

Respond to Questions on Step 2 Sources

These questions will help you analyze the sources you've read. Use your notes and refer to the sources in order to answer the questions. Your answers to these questions will help you write your essay.

1 **Prose Constructed-Response** What does Whitman's "Letter from Paumanok" tell you about his experience of life in the United States?

What this tells me about his experiences is that he had an interesting conversation with a man and then gets interrupted by a lady. He enjoyed the conversation - meeting people and enjoys that human interaction.

2 **Prose Constructed-Response** What insights do you gain into Whitman's experiences as a Civil War nurse from reading his letter to his mother?

Whitman is describing how he's keeping the wounded soldier company. He's seen the war as depressing and he realized that life wasn't easy.

3 **Prose Constructed-Response** What evidence of Whitman's life experiences do you see in "I Hear America Singing"? Cite specific details from the poem and the other sources.

He finds pride in the work that different people do. "I hear America singing, the varied carols I hear" All these people working creates harmony

4 **Prose Constructed-Response** What evidence of Whitman's life experiences do you see in "The Real War Will Never Get in the Books"? Cite specific details from the journal entry and the other sources.

Whitman is explaining how the war is like hell - and noone writes the truth about the wars. It states in Lines 1-4 - it supports his experience. No one sees the things people go through

Planning and Prewriting

When you take a biographical approach to literary criticism, you analyze details in the literature that reflect details from the writer's life experiences.

 You may prefer to do your planning on the computer.

Analyze the Sources

Summarize what you learned about Whitman's life from each of the biographical sources. Then identify details in the poem and the journal entry that reflect those ideas.

Biographical Source	Ideas About Whitman's Life	Related Details from Poem and/or Journal Entry
Biography: Walt Whitman	• 1819 - 1892 • grew in NY, Brooklyn, Long Island • he plied many trades (journalist, printer etc) • witnessed slavery in New Orleans • kept writing that could transform his life	"he put his journalistic talent to work at the New Orleans Crescent while observing the brutal force of slavery"
Newspaper Article: Letter from Paumanok	• interested with talking to the guy • asked him questions back • had fun with the social interactions	no "I thought it more than fair to return the compliment in kind, and so pitched into him"
Letter: Letter to His Mother	• told her about his experiences • wounded soldier with a big heart! • he was a nurse and helped	"he likes to have some one to talk to and we will listen to him, he got badly wounded in the leg and side"

Develop Your Essay

A literary analysis is an examination of a specific aspect of a text. An essayist may put forward an argument or an interpretation of the text.

Determine the Topic

After a thoughtful reading of a text, an essayist chooses one particular aspect to analyze. This becomes the topic of the essay. For the essay you are writing, you are specifically being asked to write on the following topic: the ways in which Whitman's life experiences are reflected in his writings.

Write the Claim or Central Idea

To write the claim or central idea, an essayist puts forward an assertion about the topic and comments upon its importance or significance.

The topic for the model essay in this unit was how William Stafford's life influenced his writing. Look closely at the ways in which the essayist makes an assertion and comments upon the importance or significance of her assertion. In the chart below, identify the assertion that Jennifer makes and how she explains the importance or significance of her assertion.

Jennifer's Essay
Claim: When we analyze it carefully, we also find the poet's life experiences and philosophy reflected in many of its details, including the setting, voice, and point of view. Knowing about the author's biography and his perspective on life helps us analyze his writing on a deeper level and understand it more fully.
Assertion:
Importance/Significance:

Using what you have discovered about writing a claim or central idea for a literary analysis, create your own claim for the essay you will be writing about Walt Whitman's work. Record your claim in the chart on page 103.

Choose the Structure and Craft the Key Points

Essayists choose a structure that aligns to the claim or central idea and for which key points can be pulled from the text. Take a look at the way Jennifer organized her model essay. You might organize your essay similarly or invent another logical structure for your essay.

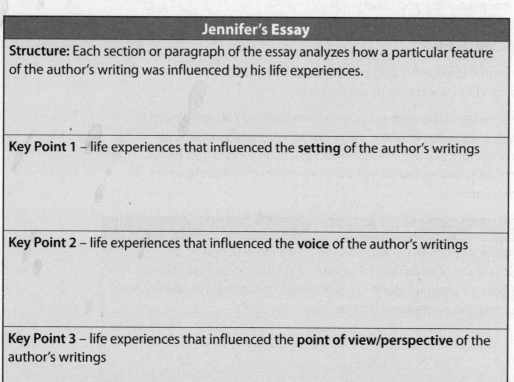

Jennifer's Essay
Structure: Each section or paragraph of the essay analyzes how a particular feature of the author's writing was influenced by his life experiences.
Key Point 1 – life experiences that influenced the **setting** of the author's writings
Key Point 2 – life experiences that influenced the **voice** of the author's writings
Key Point 3 – life experiences that influenced the **point of view/perspective** of the author's writings

Using what you have discovered about structure and creating key points, decide on your structure and key points and record them in the following chart.

Topic
Ways in which Whitman's life experiences are reflected in his writings

Claim or Central Idea

Structure and Key Points
(List at least three key points, and more if you need them.)

Structure:

Key Point 1:

Key Point 2:

Key Point 3:   central idea:
Everyone has a role in society

Key Point 4:

Key Point 5:

Collect Textual Evidence

Once an essayist has determined both the structure and the key points, the evidence to support each key point is collected. You can begin to record your evidence in the planner on page 104.

(1.) Life experiences has a big impact on your future/or life

© Houghton Mifflin Harcourt Publishing Company

Finalize Your Plan

Use your responses and notes from previous pages to create a detailed plan for your essay.

▶ "Hook" your audience with an interesting detail, question, quotation, or anecdote.

▶ State the central idea of your essay.

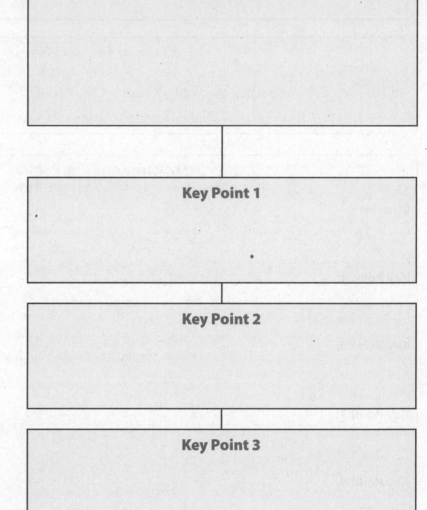

Introduction

Key Point 1

Key Point 2

Key Point 3

Conclusion

▶ Present each of your key points in a logical order.

▶ Include relevant facts, concrete details, and other evidence to support each of your points.

▶ Summarize the key points and restate your central idea.

▶ Include an insight that follows from and supports your central idea.

1. Analyze   2. Practice   3. Perform

Cite Your Sources

An authoritative literary analysis provides evidence from the literature and from other sources to support the essayist's claim or interpretation. In addition to citing sources, a literary analysis cites specific line numbers from poetry and other verse. The format used by the Modern Language Association (MLA) is demonstrated in the student model on pages 86–87.

Make Notes on Each Source Depending on the exact sources you are using, you'll need to gather certain information to use in your citations. Basic facts include the following:

▶ Author(s)

▶ Title of poem, story, article, or chapter within a longer work

▶ Publication title and type of publication (book, website, magazine, etc.)

▶ Publisher and date of publication

▶ Page numbers, if appropriate—especially for any specific text you plan to quote in your essay

▶ Line numbers for in-text citations of poetry quotations

Place Citations in the Text of Your Essay If you quote lines from prose, use quotation marks to set off the quote. If you paraphrase lines of poetry or prose, no quotation marks are needed. If you quote lines of poetry in your essay, set the lines off with quotation marks and use a slash (/) to indicate line breaks.

In-Text Citation Rules If the sentence or paragraph clearly indicates the name of the author, include only the page number in parentheses at the end of the sentence when quoting from a book, story, or article. Include only the line numbers when quoting from a poem.

> Twain begins the novel with Huck vouching for the accuracy of the story: "There was things which he stretched, but mainly he told the truth" (2).

> In his poem "Mending Wall," Robert Frost writes: "Before I built a wall I'd ask to know / What I was walling in or walling out" (32–33).

If the sentence or paragraph does not clearly indicate the name of the author, include both the author's name and the page number (or line numbers for poetry) in parentheses at the end of the sentence.

> The novel begins with Huck vouching for the accuracy of the story: "There was things which he stretched, but mainly he told the truth" (Twain 2).

> The narrator of "Mending Wall" wonders: "Before I built a wall I'd ask to know / What I was walling in or walling out" (Frost 32–33).

If you cite more than one text from the same author, provide an abbreviated title for the work to distinguish it from other works. Titles of books or long poems should be underlined or italicized; titles of short stories, short poems, and articles should be set off in quotation marks. See below for two examples of quotations from poems by Robert Frost.

> We see this challenge to the status quo in "Before I built a wall I'd ask to know / What I was walling in or walling out" ("Mending Wall" 32–33).

> "Yet knowing how way leads on to way, / I doubted if I should ever come back" reveals the permanence of decisions ("Road Not Taken" 11–12).

If you are citing from a text with no known author, use a shortened title of the work instead of the author's name and provide a page number.

> "On the pages of books, we embark on quests, discover treasure, and are forever changed without ever leaving the sofa" ("Why Read" 52).

Create Your "Works Cited" List Use the following bulleted points to help organize and format your list:

▶ List all the sources you have used in your essay in a Works Cited list.

▶ Authors are listed with their last names first. The list is then arranged by alphabetical order of the first word in each entry.

▶ Check with your teacher about including URLs for websites, which the MLA considers optional.

▶ Use these guidelines for citing the sources on pages 90–98:

Website	Author(s) (if available). "Title of Page." *Name of Site.* Sponsor or publisher of website (usually an organization or company), date of publication (if available). Medium of publication (Web). Date of access.
Book	Author(s). *Title of Book.* City of publication: Publisher, Year of publication. Medium of publication (Print).

Get Help Online If you have Internet access, citation generators can help you get the format of your Works Cited list just right. Search for "MLA citation generators" or try one of the sites suggested at http://mlaformat.org/mla-format-generator/.

Draft Your Essay

As you write, think about:

▶ **Audience:** Your teacher and your classmates

▶ **Purpose:** Demonstrate your understanding of the specific requirements of a literary analysis that takes a biographical approach to literary criticism.

▶ **Style:** Use a formal and objective tone.

▶ **Transitions:** Use words and phrases such as *for example, as illustrated by,* and *is reflected in* to show how your text evidence supports your key points.

Revise

Revision Checklist: Self Evaluation

Use the checklist below to guide your analysis.

 If you drafted your essay on the computer, you may wish to print it out so that you can more easily evaluate it.

Ask Yourself	Tips	Revision Strategies
1. Does the introduction get the readers' attention and include a clear central idea? ✓	Draw a line under the compelling introductory text. Circle the central idea.	Add a compelling introductory sentence or idea. Make your central idea clear and precise.
2. Are there clearly stated key points about how Whitman's life is reflected in his writing? Are all key points supported by textual evidence?	Underline the key points. Circle the textual evidence that supports each point.	Revise any key points that are unclear or confusing. Add evidence so that each point is thoroughly supported.
3. Are points presented in a logical order with clear and varied transitions between related ideas?	Identify the logic of the structure, such as order of importance or order of appearance in the literary work. Put check marks next to transitions that link the points.	Rearrange body paragraphs to present points in a logical order. Add varied transitions to connect ideas as needed.
4. Is there a strong conclusion? Does it give the reader insight into Whitman's life and writing?	Put a plus sign beside the concluding statement. Star the text that supports the conclusion. Underline the insight that is offered to readers.	Add an overarching view of key points or a final observation about Whitman's life and writing.
5. Are sources cited both within the text and in a Works Cited list?	Highlight specific facts, details, and quotations taken from the literature and other sources.	Add in-text citations as needed. Revise the Works Cited list to correct any formatting errors.

Revision Checklist: Peer Review

Exchange your essay with a classmate, or read it aloud to your partner. As you read and comment on your classmate's essay, focus on how it demonstrates the connections between Whitman's life and writing. Help each other identify parts of the draft that need strengthening, reworking, or a new approach.

What To Look For	Notes for My Partner
1. Does the ~~introduction grab~~ the audience's attention and include a clear central idea?	The central idea is clear and you provided evidence/supporting detail in order to back up the central idea.
2. Are there clearly stated key points about how Whitman's life is reflected in his writing? Are all key points supported by textual evidence?	All key points are clear and supported with textual evidence.
3. Are points presented in a logical order with clear and varied transitions between related ideas?	Points are presented in logical order and not all over, one point is focused on before transitioning to the next.
⟍4. Is there a strong conclusion that follows from or is supported by the preceding paragraphs? Does it give the reader something to think about?	
5. Are sources cited within the text ~~and in a Works Cited list?~~	Sources are cited in the text, so evidence can be found in the right texts.

Edit

 Edit your essay to correct spelling, grammar, and punctuation errors.

How do our life experiences change us?

You will read:

▶ **A BIOGRAPHY**
The Life of Elizabeth Barrett Browning

▶ **A HISTORICAL ESSAY**
The Browning Letters

▶ **A POEM**
"Sonnet 43"

▶ **TWO LETTERS**
The Letters of Robert Browning and Elizabeth Barrett Barrett

You will write:

▶ **A LITERARY ANALYSIS**
How did Elizabeth Barrett Browning's life experiences influence her poetry?

The Life of
Elizabeth Barrett Browning

by Alicia Kim

AS YOU READ *Focus on the facts and details in this biographical essay that explain how Elizabeth Barrett Browning's life and emotional attachment to Robert Browning influenced her writing. Record comments or questions about the text in the side margins.*

NOTES

Born in 1806 in Durham, England, Elizabeth Barrett Browning was an English poet who gained enormous fame during her lifetime. The oldest of twelve children, she was born into great wealth, her father having made most of his fortune from sugar plantations that he owned in Jamaica. By all accounts, Elizabeth lived a privileged childhood, riding her pony around the grounds of her family's estate and visiting the local neighbors. Educated at home, she was something of a child prodigy. She writes that at age six she was reading novels. At age ten she was studying Greek, writing
10 her own epic poem in the Greek style two years later.

While living with her father in London, Elizabeth published her first book of mature poetry, which gained her some fame. Her book *The Seraphim and Other Poems* (1838) borrowed styles from Greek tragedy but used them to express her deep Christian faith. During these years in London, her father sent some of his other children to Jamaica to help manage the family plantations, which were losing money. Elizabeth was a fierce opponent of slavery and hated for her siblings to be involved in it. At the same time, her ill health (the exact cause of which is unknown) worsened, forcing her to spend a year on
20 the coast with her favorite brother, Edward. He tragically drowned a year later. Distraught over Edward's death, Elizabeth returned home, becoming an invalid and a recluse. She spent the next five years in her bedroom in the house on Wimpole Street, seeing few people.

Elizabeth continued to write, and in 1844 published a volume of poetry with the simple title of *Poems*. This book made her one of the most popular writers in England, and it gained the attention of

the renowned poet Robert Browning, whose work she had praised in one of her poems. After reading these poems, Browning wrote to her, saying, "I LOVE your verses with all my heart, dear Miss Barrett,"
30 and so begins one of the greatest love stories in literary history.

As their correspondence continued, the couple exchanged nearly 600 letters, falling in love and marrying secretly on September 12, 1846. Although most of her family accepted the marriage, Elizabeth's father disowned her, refusing to open her letters or to see her. Edward Moulton-Barrett has been described as a devoted father, and he may have felt that Robert lacked the resources to support his daughter. However, he did not take kindly to disobedience, and he also disowned two of Elizabeth's siblings who married without his permission.

40 Out of the romantic courtship between Elizabeth Barrett and Robert Browning came an outpouring of love, which Elizabeth transformed into poetry. In 1849 she gave Robert a small packet of these sonnets, which she had written to him in secret before their marriage. Her husband decided to publish them, saying that he could not keep these poems to himself, for they were "the finest sonnets written in the English language since Shakespeare's." In 1850 the poems appeared as *Sonnets from the Portuguese* and included Elizabeth's most famous love poem to Robert, "Sonnet 43," written in 1845 or 1846. It begins, "How do I love thee? Let me count the
50 ways."

Moving to Italy after their marriage, the Brownings and their son spent many happy years there, until Elizabeth passed away, dying in Robert's arms, on June 29, 1861. Of their profound love and poetry, their friend and literary critic Frederic Kenyon wrote that "no modern English poet has written of love with such genius, such beauty, and such sincerity, as the two who gave the most beautiful example of it in their own lives."

From *Poetry and Life* (New York: Short Press, 1994), pages 31–32.

Discuss and Decide

With a small group, discuss how Elizabeth Barrett Browning's life and experiences provide a context for her work. Cite text evidence in your discussion.

Source 2: Historical Essay

The Browning Letters

by Gregory Evans

AS YOU READ *Pay close attention to the details describing the love letters written and received by the Victorian poets Robert Browning and Elizabeth Barrett. Pay special attention to the historical context in which they were written.*

NOTES

No story of the great Victorian poets Elizabeth Barrett Browning (1806–1861) and Robert Browning (1812–1889) could be told without providing a close reading of their love letters to each other, 574 letters in all, written between January 10, 1845, and September 18, 1846. Beginning with a letter addressed to "dear Miss Barrett" and ending with Elizabeth's note to Robert as they arranged to leave England and travel to Italy a week after their marriage, the love letters of Robert Browning and Elizabeth Barrett are among the most famous in literary history, providing meaningful insights into their lives, 10 love, thoughts, feelings, experiences, and poetry.

After reading her poems for the first time, Robert Browning begins the correspondence with the line: "I LOVE your verses with all my heart, dear Miss Barrett," describing the poems as "fresh strange music" and transferring his love for her poetry into love for her before the end of the letter: "I do, as I say, love these books with all my heart—and I love you too." With that first meeting of their hearts and minds, a love affair blossoms between them. As their correspondence deepens over the course of twenty months, Elizabeth tells an acquaintance that they "are growing to be the truest of 20 friends." Yet by January 10, 1846, exactly one year after Robert's first letter, the friendship that Elizabeth has felt for him has clearly turned to love.

Elizabeth writes:

> Do you know, when you have told me to think of you, I
> have been feeling ashamed of thinking of you so much,
> of thinking of only you—which is too much
> perhaps. . . . Shall I tell you? It seems to me, to myself,
> that no man was ever before to any woman what you
> are to me. . . .

The rest, as they say, is history, as the most romantic literary couple of the Victorian era falls in love through their letters and secretly marries on September 12, 1846.

30   Of course, the Browning letters are not the only series of love letters that have survived the centuries. Letters written by Henry VIII to Anne Boleyn, by the poet John Keats to his beloved Fanny Brawne, and by Abigail Adams to her husband, John Adams, are other notable examples. Despite the different people writing them, all these love letters have the same purpose—to sweep the recipient off his or her feet by a frank, even poetic, display of feelings.

    Yet the fact that the Browning letters were written by two literary giants attests to the letters' uniqueness. Perhaps only poets can write of love in this way, using metaphors and symbols, making the
40 Browning letters unparalleled for their beauty, sincerity, and deeply poetic display of emotion.

Posted February 14, 2013, at *Letters for the Ages* website.

Close Read

Summarize the article you have just read. How did Elizabeth Barrett and Robert Browning fall in love? Cite text evidence in your response.

_____

_____

_____

_____

_____

Source 3: Poem

Background: *Elizabeth Barrett wrote this sonnet sometime in 1845 or 1846, during her courtship with Robert Browning.*

Sonnet 43

by Elizabeth Barrett Browning

AS YOU READ *Focus on the form of this sonnet, a 14-line poem with a definite rhyme scheme and meter. Record comments or questions about the text in the side margin.*

NOTES

How do I love thee? Let me count the ways.

I love thee to the depth and breadth and height

My soul can reach, when feeling out of sight

For the ends of Being and ideal Grace.

5 I love thee to the level of everyday's

Most quiet need, by sun and candlelight.

I love thee freely, as men strive for Right;

I love thee purely, as they turn from Praise.

I love thee with passion put to use

10 In my old griefs, and with my childhood's faith.

I love thee with a love I seemed to lose

With my lost saints,—I love thee with the breath,

Smiles, tears, of all my life!—and, if God choose,

I shall but love thee better after death.

From *Sonnets from the Portuguese* (Portland, ME: Thomas B. Mosher, 1910), page 45.

Close Read

Reread the last six lines of the poem. How is the poet comparing the intensity of love she feels for Robert Browning with the intensity of love she had experienced earlier in her life? Cite text evidence in your response.

_____

_____

THE LETTERS OF
Robert Browning AND
Elizabeth Barrett Barrett

R.B. to E.B.B.

New Cross, Hatcham, Surrey.
[Post-mark, January 10, 1845.]

I LOVE your verses with all my heart, dear Miss Barrett,—and
this is no off-hand complimentary letter that I shall write,—
whatever else, no prompt matter-of-course recognition of your
genius, and there a graceful and natural end of the thing. Since
the day last week when I first read your poems, I quite laugh to
remember how I have been turning and turning again in my mind
what I should be able to tell you of their effect upon me, for in the
first flush of delight I thought I would this once get out of my habit
of purely passive enjoyment, when I do really enjoy, and thoroughly
10 justify my admiration—perhaps even, as a loyal fellow-craftsman
should, try and find fault and do you some little good to be proud
of hereafter!—but nothing comes of it all—so into me has it gone,
and part of me has it become, this great living poetry of yours, not
a flower of which but took root and grew. Oh, how different that is
from lying to be dried and pressed flat, and prized highly, and put
in a book with a proper account at top and bottom, and shut up and
put away . . . and the book called a 'Flora,' besides! After all, I need
not give up the thought of doing that, too, in time; because even
now, talking with whoever is worthy, I can give a reason for my faith
20 in one and another excellence, the fresh strange music, the affluent
language, the exquisite pathos and true new brave thought; but in
this addressing myself to you—your own self, and for the first time,
my feeling rises altogether. I do, as I say, love these books with all
my heart—and I love you too. Do you know I was once not very far

AS YOU READ *As you read
these letters, note passages or
details that you find especially
powerful.*

NOTES

from seeing—really seeing you? Mr. Kenyon said to me one morning 'Would you like to see Miss Barrett?' then he went to announce me,—then he returned . . . you were too unwell, and now it is years ago, and I feel as at some untoward passage in my travels, as if I had been close, so close, to some world's-wonder in chapel or crypt, only 30 a screen to push and I might have entered, but there was some slight, so it now seems, slight and just sufficient bar to admission, and the half-opened door shut, and I went home my thousands of miles, and the sight was never to be?

Well, these Poems were to be, and this true thankful joy and pride with which I feel myself,

Yours ever faithfully,
ROBERT BROWNING.

E.B.B. to R.B.

50 Wimpole Street: Jan. 11, 1845.

I thank you, dear Mr. Browning, from the bottom of my heart. You meant to give me pleasure by your letter—and even if the object had not been answered, I ought still to thank you. But it is thoroughly answered. Such a letter from such a hand! Sympathy is dear—very dear to me: but the sympathy of a poet, and of such a poet, is the quintessence of sympathy to me! Will you take back my gratitude for it?—agreeing, too, that of all the commerce done in the world, from Tyre to Carthage,[1] the exchange of sympathy for gratitude is the most princely thing! . . .

10   Is it indeed true that I was so near to the pleasure and honour of making your acquaintance? and can it be true that you look back upon the lost opportunity with any regret? *But*—you know—if you had entered the 'crypt,' you might have caught cold, or been tired to death, and *wished* yourself 'a thousand miles off;' which would have been worse than travelling them. It is not my interest, however,

---

[1] **Tyre to Carthage:** According to ancient Greek sources, a princess of Tyre named Dido flees to Carthage after her husband is murdered. She makes a clever bargain to buy all of Carthage and becomes its queen.

to put such thoughts in your head about its being 'all for the best'; and I would rather hope (as I do) that what I lost by one chance I may recover by some future one. Winters shut me up as they do dormouse's eyes; in the spring, *we shall see*: and I am so much better

20 that I seem turning round to the outward world again. And in the meantime I have learnt to know your voice, not merely from the poetry but from the kindness in it. Mr. Kenyon often speaks of you— dear Mr. Kenyon!—who most unspeakably, or only speakably with tears in my eyes,—has been my friend and helper, and my book's friend and helper! critic and sympathiser, true friend of all hours! You know him well enough, I think, to understand that I must be grateful to him.

I am writing too much,—and notwithstanding that I am writing too much, I will write of one thing more. I will say that I am your

30 debtor, not only for this cordial letter and for all the pleasure which came with it, but in other ways, and those the highest: and I will say that while I live to follow this divine art of poetry, in proportion to my love for it and my devotion to it, I must be a devout admirer and student of your works. This is in my heart to say to you—and I say it.

And, for the rest, I am proud to remain

Your obliged and faithful
ELIZABETH B. BARRETT.

From *The Letters of Robert Browning and Elizabeth Barrett Browning,* Vol. 1, edited by Robert Browning (London: Smith, Elder, & Co., 1900), pages 1–8.

Discuss and Decide

With a small group, discuss the content and tone of each letter. In what ways are they similar? Cite text evidence in your discussion.

Respond to Questions on Step 3 Sources

These questions will help you think about the essays, the poem, and the letters you have read. Use your notes and refer to the sources in order to answer the questions. Your answers will help you write your essay.

1 **Prose Constructed-Response** What comparisons about the poet's love for Robert Browning and her religious and political beliefs does she make in the first eight lines of the sonnet? Cite specific evidence from the text.

_____

_____

_____

_____

2 **Prose Constructed-Response** How are the last six lines of the poem influenced by Elizabeth Barrett Browning's life experiences?

_____

_____

_____

_____

3 **Prose Constructed-Response** How does the essay about the Browning letters help you place the two letters you have read in both a historical and a personal context?

_____

_____

_____

_____

Part 2: Write

ASSIGNMENT

Write a literary analysis considering the ways in which Elizabeth Barrett Browning's life experiences influenced her writing of "Sonnet 43." Support your central idea with evidence from the texts.

Plan

Use the graphic organizer to help you outline the structure of your literary analysis.

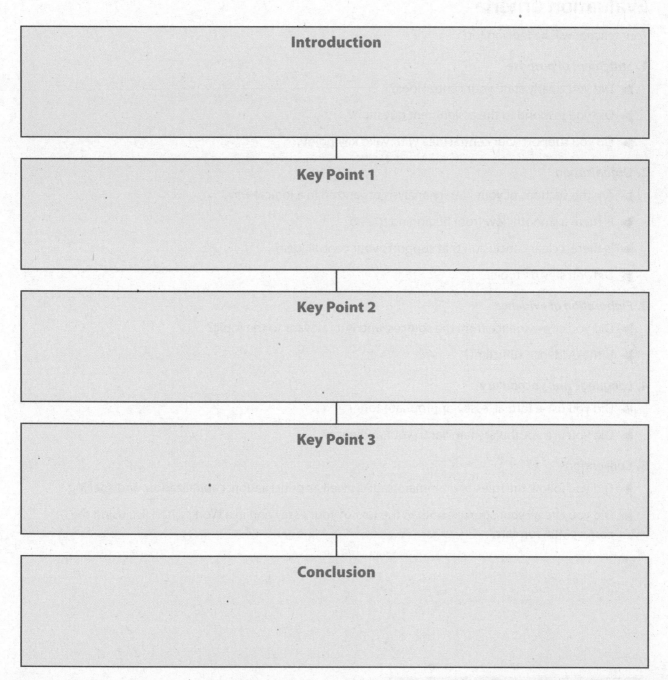

Introduction

Key Point 1

Key Point 2

Key Point 3

Conclusion

Draft

 Use your notes and completed graphic organizer to write a first draft of your
literary analysis.

Revise and Edit

 Look back over your essay and compare it to the Evaluation Criteria.
Revise your literary analysis and edit it to correct spelling, grammar, and
punctuation errors.

Evaluation Criteria

Your teacher will be looking for:

1. *Statement of purpose*

▶ Did you clearly state your central idea?

▶ Did you respond to the assignment question?

▶ Do you support your central idea with valid key points?

2. *Organization*

▶ Are the sections of your literary analysis organized in a logical way?

▶ Is there a smooth flow from beginning to end?

▶ Is there a clear conclusion that supports your central idea?

▶ Did you stay on topic?

3. *Elaboration of evidence*

▶ Did you cite evidence from the sources, and is it relevant to the topic?

▶ Is the evidence sufficient?

4. *Language and vocabulary*

▶ Did you use a formal, essay-appropriate tone?

▶ Did you use vocabulary familiar to your audience?

5. *Conventions*

▶ Did you follow the rules of grammar usage as well as punctuation, capitalization, and spelling?

▶ Did you cite all your sources, both in the text of your essay and in a Works Cited list, using the
correct MLA formats?

On Your Own

Time Management: Argumentative Task

TASK 1

RESEARCH SIMULATION

Argumentative Essay

Your Assignment

You will read three articles about government regulation of food and drink. Then you will write an argumentative essay in which you take a position on the topic.

Time Management: Argumentative Task

There are two parts to most formal writing tests. Both parts of the tests are timed, so it's important to use your limited time wisely.

Part 1: Read Sources

Preview the articles as you check how many pages you will be reading. This will give you an overview of the contents and help you identify important information.

This is a lot to do in a short time.

Preview the Assignment

35 minutes

You will have 35 minutes to read three articles about government regulation of food and drink. You will then write an essay on the topic.

How many?

35 minutes! That's not much time.

How many pages of reading?

How do you plan to use the 35 minutes?

Underline, circle, and take notes as you read. You probably won't have time to reread.

Estimated time to read:

"Sugary Drinks over 16-Ounces Banned in New York City…"   minutes

"Food Politics"   minutes

"Should the Government Regulate What We Eat?"   minutes

Total   35   minutes

Any concerns?

_____

_____

_____

_____

_____

Part 2: Write the Essay

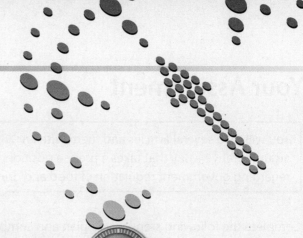

85

How much time do you have? Pay attention to the clock!

Plan and Write an Argumentative Essay

85 minutes

You will have 85 minutes to plan, write, revise, and edit your essay.

Your Plan

Before you start to write, decide on your precise claim. Then think about the evidence you will use to support your claim.

How do you plan to use the 85 minutes?

Be sure to leave enough time for this step.

Estimated time for planning the essay?		minutes
Estimated time for writing?		minutes
Estimated time for revising?		minutes
Estimated time for editing, including checking spelling, grammar, and punctuation?		minutes
Total	**85**	**minutes**

Notes:

_____

_____

_____

_____

_____

_____

Reread your essay, making sure that the points are clear. Check that there are no spelling or punctuation mistakes.

► Your Assignment

> You will read several articles and then write an argumentative essay that takes a precise position regarding government regulation of food and drink.

Complete the following steps as you plan and compose your essay.

1. Read a news report on the ban of sugary drinks in New York City.

2. Read a column about the effectiveness of regulations on food and drink.

3. Read a news report on recent attempts of the government to combat obesity.

4. Plan, write, and revise your essay.

► Part 1 (35 minutes)

As you read the sources, take notes on important facts and details. You may want to refer to your notes while planning and writing your essay.

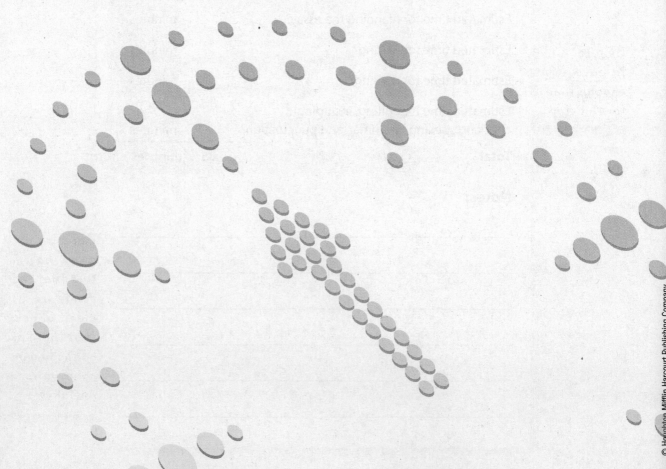

Sugary Drinks over 16-Ounces Banned in New York City, Board of Health Votes

by Ryan Jaslow, CBS News   *September 13, 2012*   **CBSNews.com**

Large sugary drinks are on their way out of New York City restaurants. New York City's Board of Health today passed a rule banning super-sized, sugary drinks at restaurants, concession stands and other eateries.

The ban passed Thursday will place a limit of 16-ounces on bottles and cups of sugar-containing sodas and other non-diet sweetened beverages beginning in March 2013.

The ban will apply in restaurants, fast-food chains, theaters, delis, office cafeterias and most other places that fall under the
10   Board of Health's regulation. People who buy sugary drinks at such establishments will still have an option to purchase an additional 16-ounce beverage.

Exempt from the ban are sugary drinks sold at supermarkets or most convenience stores and alcoholic and dairy-based beverages sold at New York City eateries.

City health officials called for the ban to combat the obesity epidemic. According to the NYC Department of Health and Mental Hygiene, more than half of adults are overweight or obese and nearly one in five kindergarten students are obese.

20   The restaurant and beverage industries have slammed the plan in ad campaigns and through public debates. The American Beverage Association has previously criticized that soda is being targeted as a culprit in the obesity epidemic over other factors.

"It's sad that the board wants to limit our choices," Liz Berman, business owner and chairwoman of New Yorkers for Beverage Choices, said in an emailed statement to CBSNews.com. "We are smart enough to make our own decisions about what to eat and drink."

Some medical professionals applauded the ban.

30   "For the past several years, I've seen the number of children and adults struggling with obesity skyrocket, putting them at early risk of

diabetes, heart disease, and cancer," Dr. Steven Safyer, President and CEO of Montefiore Medical Center, said in an emailed statement to CBSNews.com. "This policy is a great step in the battle to turn this health crisis around."

Nutritionist Karen Congro, director of the Wellness for Life Program at the Brooklyn Hospital Center, told CBSNews.com, "There are pockets of the population who have no idea what a proper serving size is, so this will help rein them in." However she added
40 without educating New Yorkers about obesity risks, the ban may not be as effective as officials hope, given people will still be able to buy sugary drinks such as Big Gulps at 7-11 convenience stores.

"Unless they get the educational portion along with it, they won't understand why it's being a banned and how it relates to them personally," Congro said.

Some New Yorkers have ridiculed the rule as a gross government intrusion.

"This is not the end," Eliot Hoff, spokesman for New Yorkers for Beverage Choices, said in a statement to CBSNews.com. "We are
50 exploring legal options, and all other avenues available to us. We will continue to voice our opposition to this ban and fight for the right of New Yorkers to make their own choices."

Am I on Track?

Actual Time Spent Reading

Food Politics

San Francisco Chronicle

In these columns from the San Francisco Chronicle, *Marion Nestle, a nutrition and public policy expert, answers readers' questions about food regulation.*

Soda-Size Cap Is a Public Health Issue
February 1, 2013

Q: You view New York City's cap on any soda larger than 16 ounces as good for public health. I don't care if sodas are bad for us. The question is "Whose choice is it?" And what role should the nanny state play in this issue?

A: As an advocate for public health, I think a soda cap makes sense. Sixteen ounces provides two full servings, about 50 grams of sugars, and 200 calories—10 percent of daily calories for someone who consumes 2,000 calories a day.

10 That's a generous amount. In the 1950s, Coca-Cola advertised this size as large enough to serve three people.

You may not care whether sodas are bad for health, but plenty of other people do. These include, among others, officials who must spend taxpayer dollars to care for the health of people with obesity-related chronic illnesses, employers dealing with a chronically ill workforce, the parents and teachers of overweight children, dentists who treat tooth decay, and a military desperate for recruits who can meet fitness standards.

Poor health is much more than an individual, personal problem. If you are ill, your illness has consequences for others.

20 That is where public health measures come in. The closest analogy is food fortification. You have to eat vitamins and iron with your bread and cereals whether you want to or not. You have to wear seat belts in a car and a helmet on a motorcycle. You can't drive much over the speed limit or under the influence. You can't smoke in public places.

Would you leave it up to individuals to do as they please in these instances regardless of the effects of their choices on themselves, other people and society? Haven't these "nanny state" measures, as you call them, made life healthier and safer for everyone?

NOTES

All the soda cap is designed to do is to make the default food choice
the healthier choice. This isn't about denial of choice. If you want
more than 16 ounces, no government official is stopping you from
ordering as many of those sizes as you like.

What troubles me about the freedom-to-choose, nanny-state
argument is that it deflects attention from the real issue: the
ferocious efforts of the soda industry to protect sales of its products
at any monetary or social cost.

Regulations Do Change Eating Behavior
August 31, 2012

**Q: I still don't get it. Why would a city government think that
food regulations would promote health when any one of them is so
easy to evade?**

A: Quick answer: because they work.

Regulations make it easier for people to eat healthfully without
having to think about it. They make the default choice the healthy
choice. Most people choose the default, no matter what it is. Telling
people cigarettes cause cancer hardly ever got anyone to stop. But
regulations did. Taxing cigarettes, banning advertising, setting
age limits for purchases, and restricting smoking in airplanes,
workplaces, bars and restaurants made it easier for smokers to
stop. Economists say, obesity and its consequences cost our society
$190 billion annually in health care and lost productivity, so health
officials increasingly want to find equally effective strategies to
discourage people from over-consuming sugary drinks and fast food.

Research backs up regulatory approaches. We know what makes
us overeat: billions of dollars in advertising messages, food sold
everywhere—in gas stations, vending machines, libraries and stores
that sell clothing, books, office supplies, cosmetics and drugs—and
huge portions of food at bargain prices.

Research also shows what sells food to kids: cartoons, celebrities,
commercials on their favorite television programs, and toys in Happy
Meals. This kind of marketing induces kids to want the products,
pester their parents for them, and throw tantrums if parents say no.
Marketing makes kids think they are supposed to eat advertised
foods, and so undermines parental authority.

Public health officials look for ways to intervene, given their
particular legislated mandates and authority. But much as they

might like to, they can't do much about marketing to children. Food and beverage companies invoke the First Amendment to protect their "right" to market junk foods to kids. They lobby Congress on this issue so effectively that they even managed to block the Federal Trade Commission's proposed nonbinding, voluntary nutrition standards for
70 marketing food to kids.

Short of marketing restrictions, city officials are trying other options. They pass laws to require menu labeling for fast food, ban trans fats, prohibit toys in fast-food kids' meals and restrict junk foods sold in schools. They propose taxes on sodas and caps on soda sizes.

Research demonstrating the value of regulatory approaches is now pouring in.

Studies of the effects of menu labeling show that not everyone pays attention, but those who do are more likely to reduce their calorie purchases. Menu labels certainly change my behavior. Do I really want
80 a 600-calorie breakfast muffin? Not today, thanks.

New York City's 2008 ban on use of hydrogenated oils containing trans fats means that New Yorkers get less trans fat with their fast food, even in low-income neighborhoods. Whether this reduction accounts for the recent decline in the city's rates of heart disease remains to be demonstrated, but getting rid of trans fats certainly hasn't hurt.

Canadian researchers report that kids are three times more likely to choose healthier meals if those meals come with a toy and the regular ones do not. When it comes to kids' food choices, the meal with the toy is invariably the default.

90 A recent study in *Pediatrics* compared obesity rates in kids living in states with and without restrictions on the kinds of foods sold in schools. Guess what—the kids living in states where schools don't sell junk food are not as overweight.

Circulation has just published an American Heart Association review of "evidence-based population approaches" to improving diets. It concludes that evidence supports the value of intense media campaigns, on-site educational programs in stores, subsidies for fruits and vegetables, taxes, school gardens, worksite wellness programs and restrictions on marketing to children.

100 The benefits of the approaches shown in these studies may appear small, but together they offer hope that current trends can be reversed.

Am I on Track?

Actual Time Spent Reading

Should the Government Regulate What We Eat?

by Bert Glass

In December of 2006, New York City's Board of Health voted to become the nation's first city to ban the use of trans fats in restaurants. The new law, which officially went into effect in July of 2008, aims to eliminate the artery-clogging fat used in the preparation of many popular food items around the city, including pizza, French fries, and various baked goods. However, the ban raises several interesting questions in regard to the level of government involvement in regulating what we eat. When faced with the facts about the dangers of consuming foods prepared with trans fats,

10 shouldn't it ultimately be each citizen's right to choose whether or not to consume foods prepared with the controversial item? Or is our government doing us a favor by making a universal decision to force us to find an alternative means of preparing food without the life-threatening ingredient?

Trans fats are formed when oils that are liquid at room temperature are mixed with hydrogen (a process called hydrogenation) and become solid fats. Many companies and restaurants choose to use trans fats in their food because they significantly increase the shelf life of their products. Also, trans fats

20 are instrumental in creating a specific taste and texture in many foods that some consumers find desirable. Trans fats are also much easier to transport and ship than other oils and fats due to their unique solid state. However, all of these positives come with a dark side.

Advocates that support the ban on trans fats are quick to point out the negative health effects of consuming food prepared with the banned item. For example, trans fats can raise our level of "bad" cholesterol while also lowering our "good" cholesterol levels, both of which can contribute to heart disease. Also, the artery-clogging

30 properties of trans fats can lead to a number of health problems requiring medical care, which can cost taxpayers billions of dollars each year.

The real issue at hand, however, revolves around the government's ability to regulate what we eat based on a number of unreliable health studies. Does this open the door to the government being able to regulate even the most minute details of our lives? For example, will the government soon be able to regulate what kinds of movies we're allowed to see in the theater, based on their arbitrary judgment of whether or not a film is dangerous to our mental health?
40 Will the government soon regulate our consumption of red meat, under the assumption that vegetables provide a much healthier alternative to the artery-clogging properties of a steak?

While it is easy enough to view the ban on trans fats as an isolated incident, such a ban ultimately puts the American values of freedom and individualism in jeopardy. If we no longer have the right to have a plate of French fries and a hamburger prepared with the ingredients we are used to, our American right to make informed decisions on our own without the government's intervention is in very big trouble.

From *We Are the Government* website, Government Analysis Publishing, Inc., 2006.

Am I on Track?

Actual Time Spent Reading

▶ Part 2 (85 minutes)

You now have 85 minutes to review your notes and sources and to plan, draft, revise, and edit your essay. While you may use your notes and refer to the sources, your essay must represent your original work. Now read your assignment and begin your work.

Your assignment

You have read three texts about government regulation of food and drink. The three texts are:

- "Sugary Drinks over 16-Ounces Banned in New York City, Board of Health Votes"

- "Food Politics"

- "Should the Government Regulate What We Eat?"

Consider the positions presented in each text.

Write an essay in which you take a position on government regulation of what we eat and drink. Remember to use textual evidence to support your claim.

Now begin work on your essay. Manage your time carefully so that you can:

1. plan your essay

2. write your essay

3. revise and edit your final draft

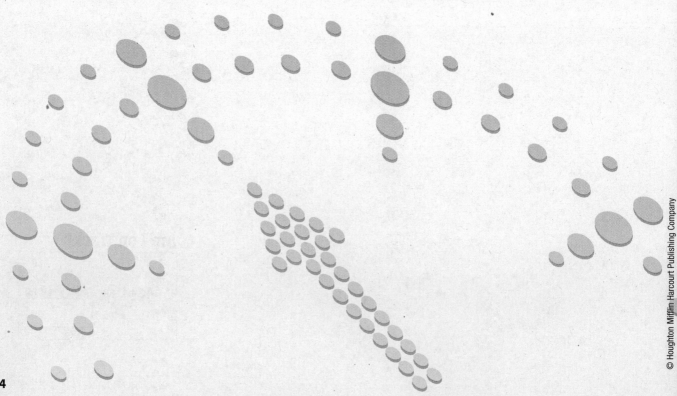

RESEARCH SIMULATION

Informative Essay

Your Assignment

You will read three selections about historic leaders. Then you will write an informative essay on the characteristics of good leaders.

Time Management: Informative Task

There are two parts to most formal writing tests. Both parts of the tests are timed, so it's important to use your limited time wisely.

Part 1: Read Sources

Preview the articles as you check how many pages you will be reading. This will give you an overview of the contents and help you identify important information.

This is a lot to do in a short time.

Preview the Assignment

35 minutes

You will have 35 minutes to read three selections about historic leaders. You will then write an essay on the topic.

How many?

How many pages of reading?

How do you plan to use the 35 minutes?

35 minutes! That's not much time.

Underline, circle, and take notes as you read. You probably won't have time to reread.

Estimated time to read:

"Suleiman the Magnificent"	minutes
"Nelson Mandela Inaugurated President of South Africa"	minutes
"Accomplishments of Queen Elizabeth I"	minutes
Total	**35 minutes**

Any concerns?

_____

_____

_____

_____

_____

_____

_____

Part 2: Write the Essay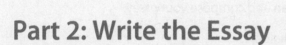

How much time do you have? Pay attention to the clock!

Plan and Write an Informative Essay

85 minutes

You will have 85 minutes to plan, write, revise, and edit your essay.

Your Plan

Before you start to write, decide on a central idea for your essay and details that support that central idea.

How do you plan to use the 85 minutes?

Estimated time for planning the essay?		minutes
Estimated time for writing?		minutes
Be sure to leave enough time for this step. Estimated time for revising?		minutes
Estimated time for editing, including checking spelling, grammar, and punctuation?		minutes
Total	**85**	**minutes**

Notes:

_____

_____

_____

_____

_____

_____

Reread your essay, making sure that the points are clear. Check that there are no spelling or punctuation mistakes.

▶ Your Assignment

> You will read three articles about historic leaders and then write an informative essay about how these people exhibit characteristics of great leaders.

Complete the following steps as you plan and compose your essay.

1. Read three selections about historic leaders.

2. Plan, write, and revise your essay.

▶ Part 1 (35 minutes)

As you read the sources, take notes on important facts and details. You may want to refer to your notes while planning and writing your essay.

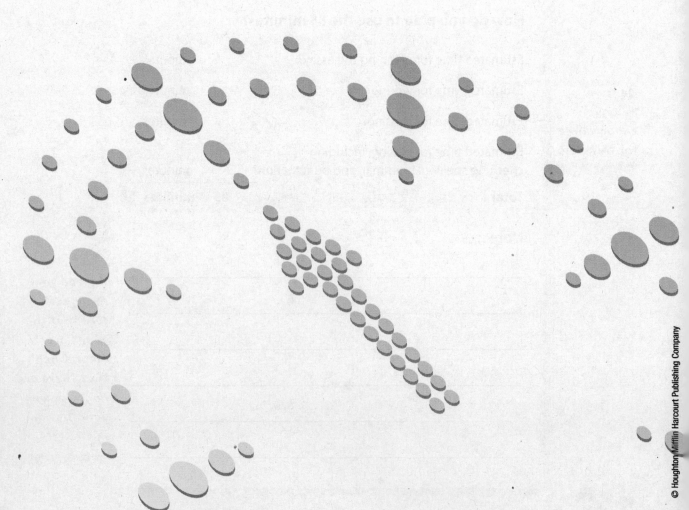

Suleiman the Magnificent

by Jane Simmons

In 1453, Ottoman armies from the western highlands of Turkey captured the city of Constantinople. They renamed the city Istanbul and made it the center of their growing empire. In 1520 a new sultan (supreme ruler) ascended the Ottoman throne. This sultan, Suleiman, became one of the greatest rulers in history. An aggressive military leader, he was feared but also admired by people in other lands. His people called him Kanuni, "the Lawgiver." Europeans called him Suleiman the Magnificent.

Suleiman the Warrior

The thunderous sound of goatskin drums and the clash of
10 brass cymbals reverberated off the great walls of the island city of Rhodes. This battle music was designed to strike fear in the hearts of its enemies. It had its intended effect. To the Greek soldiers on the ramparts, it seemed as if the very heavens had opened and let loose bolts of lightning and clashes of thunder. Even though it was extremely hot, the warriors felt a chill. After all, they were confronting the army of Suleiman the Magnificent, who had already captured the Eastern European city of Belgrade.

The drums and cymbals reached a crescendo. Suleiman's warriors raced forward to attack one of the most highly fortified
20 cities in Europe. In wave after wave they came, a hundred thousand strong. After more than 130 days of fighting, the Ottoman army entered Rhodes victorious.

Over many years, the fleets of Rhodes had intercepted Ottoman ships and disrupted its commerce. Now the routes were clear. After consolidating his victory and replenishing his army, Suleiman set his sights on other conquests. A soldier's soldier, Suleiman always rode at the head of his army to inspire his troops.

In 1526, Suleiman clashed with the Hungarian army. Leading the Hungarians into battle was their 15-year-old king, Louis II. The
30 fighting was over in a matter of hours, due to a brilliant tactical action by Suleiman. The Sultan allowed the charging Hungarians to penetrate the front lines. Then he used an enveloping maneuver to

surround them. Attacked from all sides, the Hungarians were wiped out, and their young king was killed.

Suleiman was not just a warrior. He was interested in learning, art, architecture, and the law. Under his reign the Ottoman Empire reached its peak both as a military power and as a center of culture.

Suleiman the Builder

On a hill overlooking the narrow body of water called the Bosporus stood Topkapi Palace. First built by Mehmet II, a sultan
40 who ruled before Suleiman, Topkapi had been the chief residence of the Ottoman rulers since the 1460s. Each sultan had added something to the palace complex, a tradition that was to continue for centuries after Suleiman's rule. Topkapi Palace wasn't just a home—its many chambers and outbuildings were a place where royal administrators met to run the affairs of state, soldiers trained, treasures were safely stored, and all kinds of artists lived and worked.

Ottoman architecture used elements such as domes, half-domes, arches, slim towers called minarets, and pillars. Buildings were often decorated with colorful tiles in geometric designs. Suleiman's
50 chief architect was the brilliant Mimar Sinan, whose works are still admired today. He and other architects built bridges, dams, fountains, palaces, and mosques throughout the Ottoman Empire.

Visitors to Turkey marveled at the way builders were able to complete structures so quickly, a rarity in Europe at that time. An Ottoman architect who designed a structure frequently lived to see his work finished. Historians attribute this quickness to the specialization of the workers. Ottoman records list workers such as wood sawyers to prepare the wood beams, carpenters to do the woodwork at the site, rough masons, skilled masons, quarrymen,
60 plasterers, locksmiths, brick makers, and metalworkers. Like a modern-day assembly line, each kind of worker performed one task again and again. The benefit of this system was that everyone could work with speed and efficiency.

Suleiman, Poet and Patron of the Arts

In a courtyard surrounded by date palm trees, the poet Baki recited his poetry to an enthralled audience. Poets, artists, and philosophers used the courtyards at Topkapi Palace to present their works and exchange ideas. Suleiman himself was a prolific poet and writer.

70 Under Suleiman's rule, Istanbul became one of the world's cultural centers. Suleiman created many artists' societies that were administered from Topkapi Palace. These societies provided a training system for artists. The artists were paid fairly for the work they did. The best artists, including bookbinders, jewelers, and painters, were invited to become part of the royal court.

Suleiman's Legacy

Suleiman died in 1566. He left his successors a strong empire that was one of the world's most important powers. The efficient legal system, well-organized government, and strong military that he had built served the Ottoman Empire for many generations to come.

From *Magnifying Glass on History: Anthology of Writings About Ancient Rulers,* Mauer Publishing Group, Des Moines, IA. 2000.

Am I on Track?

Actual Time Spent Reading

Nelson Mandela Inaugurated President of South Africa

by Matt Darvil   *Pretoria Daily Item*   *May 10, 1994*

NOTES

In a short but historic ceremony, Nelson Rolihlahla Mandela took the oath of office today as president of the Republic of South Africa. The ceremony took place at South Africa's main government building, in the nation's capital. Facing a crowd of 140,000, Mandela said that today's inauguration was "a common victory for justice, for peace, for human dignity." As the first black president of South Africa, the 75-year-old Mandela pledged to build "a complete, just, and lasting peace." He said, "The time for the healing of the wounds has come."

10   Vice President Al Gore led the official delegation from the United States. With him were his wife, Tipper, and First Lady Hillary Rodham Clinton. American civil rights leaders Coretta Scott King and Jesse Jackson were also part of the group. "The history we are present to witness marks a transition in the history of our world," Mr. Gore said.

Historic Election

Today's event is a result of South Africa's first "all-race" elections. In April, South Africans of every race were allowed to vote in a national election. Mandela, candidate of the African National Congress (ANC), won a landslide victory.

20   The path to the elections began more than four years ago, when President F. W. de Klerk persuaded white South Africans to work for change with black South Africans. A key part of de Klerk's plan was the release of Mandela from prison, where he had been for 27 years.

On the day of his release, Mandela spoke of the need for democratic elections: "Universal suffrage on a common voters' roll in a united, democratic, and nonracial South Africa is the only way to peace and racial harmony."

Mandela's Long Road to Freedom

Born in 1918, Nelson Mandela grew up in rural South Africa. White South Africans ruled the country, and black South Africans

30 suffered discrimination in all aspects of their lives. When Mandela was in his 30s, South Africa adopted an official policy of racial separation called *apartheid*. Mandela's battles against apartheid would put him in prison beginning in 1962.

Mandela used every opportunity he had to speak out against the injustice of white domination. "I have dedicated myself to the struggle of the African people," he declared during one of his trials. "I have cherished the ideal of a democratic and free society in which all persons live together in harmony and with equal opportunities. It is an ideal which I hope to live for and to achieve. But, if needs be, it

40 is an ideal for which I am prepared to die."

Mandela was held at the notorious Robben Island prison. Conditions were harsh—bare cells, meager food, manual labor, and scarce contact with the outside world. And yet Mandela never lost his spirit or determination. Other prisoners benefited from spending time with him, learning history and political strategy. Robben Island became known as "Mandela University."

Mandela was an international symbol of the injustice of apartheid. All over the world, people demanded, "Free Mandela!" The white leaders of South Africa began to offer him some form of

50 conditional release as early as 1985. But Mandela was not willing to accept conditions—or return to a country where he and his people still had no political rights. "Your freedom and mine cannot be separated," he told them.

When President de Klerk took office in 1989, negotiations began for South Africa's political future. Mandela was released in February 1990. The two men continued to work together to find a way to end apartheid. In 1993, they won the Nobel Peace Prize for their efforts.

Am I on Track?

Actual Time Spent Reading

Accomplishments of
Queen Elizabeth I

by Amit Carter

Compendium of British Royalty. **Manchester: Aldritch Press, 2005.**

Compendium of British Royalty. **Manchester: Aldritch Press, 2005.**

NOTES

Queen Elizabeth I has the reputation of being one of the greatest monarchs of England. The Elizabethan era is often referred to as the Golden Age of Britain. But what did "Good Queen Bess" do that made her so beloved of the English people? What were her greatest achievements?

The Major Accomplishments of Queen Elizabeth I

- She was a gifted scholar who was able to speak several languages, including Latin, Greek, French, and Italian.

- During her reign there was a widespread increase in literacy and great achievements in the arts. Great poets and playwrights, such as William Shakespeare, Edmund Spenser, Christopher Marlowe, and Sir Walter Raleigh, created works that are still greatly admired and enjoyed.

- She greatly expanded the British Empire. She financed the explorations of such great explorers as Sir Francis Drake, Sir Walter Raleigh, Sir John Hawkins, Sir Humphrey Gilbert, and Sir Richard Greenville.

- She encouraged new scientific thinking, and important men such as Sir Francis Bacon and Dr. John Dee emerged during the Elizabethan era.

- She was considered a good and wise ruler who was truly loved by her people. Her early education helped make her highly accomplished in the art of rhetoric and public relations.

- She surrounded herself with highly intelligent, loyal advisors such as Sir William Cecil, Sir Francis Walsingham, and Sir Robert Cecil who gave her sound political advice.

- A small fleet of British navy ships, with the help of some armed merchant vessels, defeated a much larger Spanish Armada.

Am I on Track?

Actual Time Spent Reading

▶ Part 2 (85 minutes)

You now have 85 minutes to review your notes and sources and to plan, draft, revise, and edit your essay. While you may use your notes and refer to the texts, your essay must represent your original work. Now read your assignment and begin your work.

Your assignment

You have read three texts about historical leaders. Each text provides information about these leaders and their accomplishments.
The three texts are:

• "Suleiman the Magnificent"

• "Nelson Mandela Inaugurated President of South Africa"

• "Accomplishments of Queen Elizabeth I"

Consider the information presented in each text.

Write an informative essay in which you explain how each of these people exhibit leadership qualities.

Now begin work on your essay. Manage your time carefully so that you can:

1. plan your essay

2. write your essay

3. revise and edit your final draft

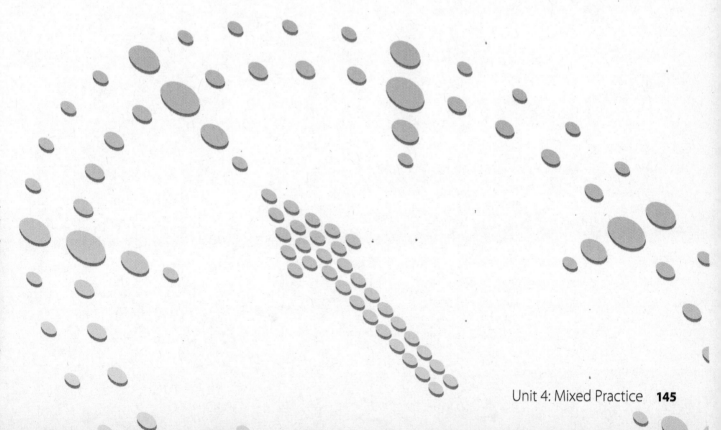

TASK 3

Literary Analysis

Your Assignment

You will read and take notes on two texts—a biography of the poet Robert Frost, and his poem "Out, Out—." Then you will use a biographical approach to literature in analyzing Frost's poem.

Time Management: Literary Analysis Task

Most formal writing tests are made up of two parts. Both parts of the tests are timed, so it's important to use your limited time wisely.

Part 1: Read Sources

Preview the Assignment

35 minutes

You will have 35 minutes to read two selections, one about Robert Frost and the other a poem by him. You will then write an essay on the topic.

35 minutes! That's not much time.

Preview the questions so you'll know which information you'll need to find as you read.

How many?

How many pages of reading?

How many prose constructed-response questions?

How do you plan to use the 35 minutes?

This is a lot to do in a short time.

Estimated time to read:

"A Biography: Robert Frost" _____ minutes

"Out, Out—" _____ minutes

Estimated time to reread:

"Taking a Biographical Approach to Literary Criticism" (page 90) _____ minutes

Estimated time to answer questions? _____ minutes

Total   **35   minutes**

Underline, circle, and take notes as you read. You probably won't have time to reread the Frost selections.

Any concerns?

_____

_____

_____

_____

_____

Part 2: Write the Analysis

85

How much time do you have? Pay attention to the clock.

Plan and Write a Literary Analysis

→ 85 minutes

You will have 85 minutes to review your notes and sources and to plan, draft, revise, and edit your essay.

Your Plan

Before you start writing, decide how you will organize your literary analysis.

How do you plan to use the 85 minutes?

Be sure to leave enough time for this step.

Estimated time for planning the essay?		minutes
Estimated time for writing?		minutes
→ Estimated time for revising?		minutes
Estimated time for editing, including checking spelling, grammar, and punctuation?		minutes
Total	**85**	**minutes**

Notes:

_____

_____

_____

_____

_____

_____

Reread your essay, making sure that the points are clear. Check that there are no spelling or punctuation mistakes.

▶ Your Assignment

You will read the two sources—a biography of the poet Robert Frost, and Frost's poem "Out, Out—." You will use these sources to write a literary analysis of "Out, Out—" using a biographical approach.

Complete the following steps as you plan and compose your essay.

1. Reread "Taking a Biographical Approach to Literary Criticism" (page 90).

2. Read a biography of Robert Frost.

3. Read the poem "Out, Out—" by Robert Frost.

4. Answer a question about the sources.

5. Plan and write your essay.

▶ Part 1 (35 minutes)

As you read the sources, take notes on important facts and details. You may want to refer to your notes while planning and writing your essay.

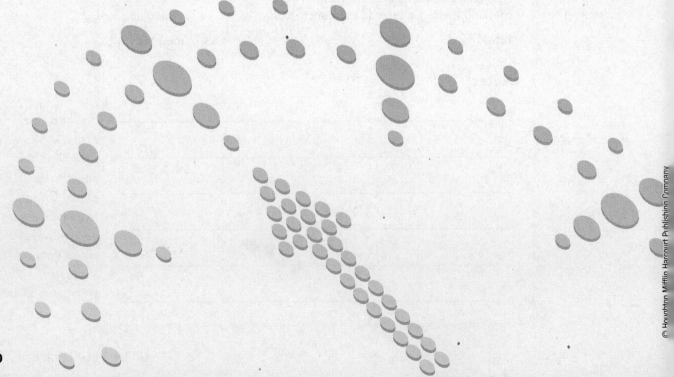

A Biography: Robert Frost

by Julio Silvera

From *Biannual Poetry Review,* MacDonald College, January 2015, page 19.

NOTES

Winner of four Pulitzer Prizes for poetry, Robert Frost (1874–1963) was for years the best-known poet in the United States. Although Frost was born in San Francisco, he was raised in New England, which became the setting for nearly all his poetry. As a young man, Frost had tried raising chickens on a farm that his grandfather had given him, but he was unsuccessful. He also had a difficult time selling his poems. In 1912, after the deaths of two of his children, he and his family moved to England. There, Frost met with success. He found a publisher for his first two collections of poems (*A Boy's Will* and *North of Boston*). The
10 books were popular immediately, and by the time Frost returned to the United States, publishers were interested in his work.

Frost lived in New England for most of his life and was known as the New England poet. He found his subjects in the landscapes and people of New England, especially in New Hampshire and Vermont. In his poems he deliberately used the everyday language he heard in conversations with farmers. The plain speech and simple, everyday subjects of his poems disguise their complex thoughts. Frost once wrote that a subject for poetry "should be common in experience and uncommon in books. . . . It should have happened to everyone but it
20 should have occurred to no one before as material."

Frost spent the rest of his long life farming, writing poetry, giving lectures, and reading his poems to audiences. As he put it, he liked to "say," rather than recite, his poetry. For example, Frost's poem "Out, Out—" is based on a real-life incident recorded in the *Littleton Courier,* a New Hampshire newspaper, on March 31, 1901, in which a boy suffers a serious accident to his hand. Frost's treatment of the subject takes into account not only the tragic story of this accident, but also Frost's own experiences. However, Frost never read this poem in public because he felt it was "too cruel." Like the title's allusion to a famous speech made
30 by Shakespeare's Macbeth upon learning of his wife's death, the poem, too, is filled with bitterness about the brevity of life—of its being a "brief candle" that can be snuffed out in an instant.

Am I on Track?

Actual Time Spent Reading

"Out, Out—"

by Robert Frost from *Mountain Interval,* pages 50–51. New York: Henry Holt and Company, 1920.

The buzz saw snarled and rattled in the yard
And made dust and dropped stove-length sticks of wood,
Sweet-scented stuff when the breeze drew across it.
And from there those that lifted eyes could count
5 Five mountain ranges one behind the other
Under the sunset far into Vermont.
And the saw snarled and rattled, snarled and rattled,
As it ran light, or had to bear a load.
And nothing happened: day was all but done.
10 Call it a day, I wish they might have said
To please the boy by giving him the half hour
That a boy counts so much when saved from work.
His sister stood beside them in her apron
To tell them "Supper." At the word, the saw,
15 As if to prove saws knew what supper meant,
Leaped out at the boy's hand, or seemed to leap—
He must have given the hand. However it was,
Neither refused the meeting. But the hand!
The boy's first outcry was a rueful laugh,
20 As he swung toward them holding up the hand,
Half in appeal, but half as if to keep
The life from spilling. Then the boy saw all—
Since he was old enough to know, big boy
Doing a man's work, though a child at heart—
25 He saw all spoiled. "Don't let him cut my hand off—
The doctor, when he comes. Don't let him, sister!"
So. But the hand was gone already.
The doctor put him in the dark of ether.
He lay and puffed his lips out with his breath.
30 And then—the watcher at his pulse took fright.
No one believed. They listened at his heart.
Little—less—nothing!—and that ended it.
No more to build on there. And they, since they
Were not the one dead, turned to their affairs.

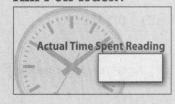

Prose Constructed-Response

Answer the following question. Your answer will be scored. You may refer to your reading notes, and you should cite text evidence in your response. You will be able to refer to your answer as you write your essay in Part 2.

Prose Constructed-Response Based on the two sources, write a paragraph that explains how taking a biographical approach to literary criticism can help you make inferences about a writer's life and how these inferences can help you interpret the text. Cite textual evidence to support your ideas.

_____

_____

_____

_____

_____

_____

_____

_____

_____

▶ Part 2 (85 minutes)

You now have 85 minutes to review your notes and sources and to plan, draft, revise, and edit your essay. While you may use your notes and refer to the sources, your essay must represent your original work. Now read your assignment and begin your work.

Your assignment

You have read two texts by or about Robert Frost. These are:

- "A Biography: Robert Frost"

- "Out, Out—"

Write a literary analysis that uses a biographical approach to analyze "Out, Out—." What elements of Robert Frost's life can you see reflected in the poem's subject and theme? Cite text evidence in your response.

Develop your essay by citing evidence from both texts. Be sure to follow the conventions of standard English.

Now begin work on your essay. Manage your time carefully so that you can:

1. plan your essay

2. write your essay

3. revise and edit your final draft

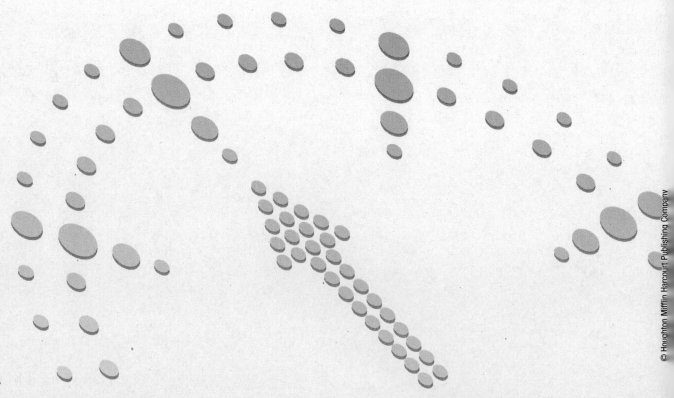

Acknowledgments

"Fifteen" from *The Way It Is: New and Selected Poems* by William Stafford. Text copyright © 1966, 1998 by the Estate of William Stafford. Reprinted by permission of the Permissions Company on behalf of the Estate of William Stafford and Graywolf Press.

"Out, Out-" from *The Poetry of Robert Frost* by Robert Frost, edited by Edward Connery Lathem. Text copyright © 1916, 1969 by Henry Holt and Company. Text copyright © 1944 by Robert Frost. Reprinted by permission of Henry Holt and Company, LLC.

Excerpt from "Regulations Do Change Eating Behavior" by Marion Nestle from *SFGate*, August 31, 2012, www.sfgate.com. Text copyright © 2012 by Marion Nestle. Reprinted by permission of Lydia Wills LLC on behalf of Marion Nestle.

"School Start Time and Sleep" from *The National Sleep Foundation*, www.sleepfoundation.org. Text copyright © 2011 by The National Sleep Foundation. Reprinted by permission of The National Sleep Foundation.

Excerpt from "Soda-Size Cap is a Public Health Issue" (Retitled: "Food Politics") by Marion Nestle from *SFGate*, February 1, 2013, www.sfgate.com. Text copyright © 2013 by Marion Nestle. Reprinted by permission of Lydia Wills LLC on behalf of Marion Nestle.

"Sugary Drinks Over 16-Ounces Banned in New York City, Board of Health Votes" by Ryan Jaslow from *CBS News*, September 13, 2012, www.cbsnews.com. Text copyright © 2012 by CBS Broadcasting, Inc. Reprinted by permission of CBS Broadcasting, Inc.

"Teenage Driving Laws May Just Delay Deadly Crashes" by Anahad O'Connor from *The New York Times*, September 14, 2011. Text copyright © 2011 by The New York Times. Reprinted by permission of PARS International on behalf of The New York Times.

"What Is a Current Event?" from *Crossing Unmarked Snow: Further Views on the Writer's Vocation* by William Stafford. Text copyright © 1998 by the University of Michigan. Reprinted by permission of the Permissions Company, Inc. on behalf of Kim Stafford.